W9-AMT-066

In the Clutches of the Kremlin: Canadian-East European Relations (1945-1962)

In the Clutches of the Kremlin: Canadian-East European Relations (1945-1962)

Aloysius Balawyder

EAST EUROPEAN MONOGRAPHS
Distributed by Columbia University Press, New York
2000

EAST EUROPEAN MONOGRAPHS, NO. DXLVI

This monograph is dedicated
to my wife, Martha, and my son, Bernard

Table of Contents

Preface

For some time, scholars lamented that there was a scarcity of scholarly publication on Canada's relations with Eastern Europe. This monograph attempts to address this problem by dealing with Canada's relations with Eastern Europe during the Cold War period. The emphasis in this study is on the bilateral relations between Canada and three East European countries, Poland, Czechoslovakia and Yugoslavia. The other three East European countries, Bulgaria, Romania and Hungary are dealt with, to a certain extent, in chapters on trade, immigration, religious persecution and psychological warfare. Canada had established with the first three countries diplomatic relations during World War II and continued them after the War. Since Bulgaria, Romania and Hungary collaborated with Nazi Germany, Canada did not establish diplomatic missions with these countries until mid-sixties.

This study approached Canadian-East European relations from the Canadian point of view. Accessibility is the reason for such an approach. The author was unable to obtain from East European archives primary sources for the period under study. On the other hand, the author was able to obtain access to departmental files located at the National Archives of Canada and at the department of External Affairs. He was also able to interview Canadian diplomats who served in the Soviet Union and/or in Eastern Europe.

The period covered in this monograph, 1945-1962, constitutes a meaningful unit. The Cold War began in earnest after World War II and continued until the coming of detente. The Cuban Crisis, 1962, initiated a respectful attitude of the super-powers for each other. A

Moscow-Washington direct line was set up to prevent a nuclear war caused by misunderstanding.

Technically, this monograph begins in 1945; however, in some chapters it deals with matter prior to this date in order to provide the reader with essential information. For instance, Chapter V summarizes Canada's immigration policy beginning in 1896. Similarly, Chapter VI has some background on Canada's commercial relations with Eastern Europe during the inter-war period. The inter-war agreements made by Canada with East European countries, formed the basis of post-World War II treaties.

This monograph was made possible with the assistance of many individuals. Piotr Staniszkis and Alice Koffyberg-Young diligently researched numerous files found at the National Archives of Canada and in the department of External Affairs files. The author is indebted to Dr. Dacre Cole, the then, public relations officer of the then Historical Division, who obtained information on various files and assisted in getting authorization to investigate External Affairs files. The author is also grateful to professors Gordon Skilling, to the late John W. Holmes, both of the University of Toronto, and to Dr. Donald Page, the dean of studies at the Trinity College, Langley, British Columbia for commenting on my earlier draft of the monograph. I am indebted to Helen MacRae, secretary of the St. Francis Xavier University Economics and History departments for conscientiously and patiently typing and retyping the monograph. I also wish to express my sincere appreciation to the Kolesars for making their computers available for me; special thanks to Patricia Kolesar for helping me to edit the manuscript and especially for methodically generating the Index. Finally, the manuscript would still be a dream if it were not for the Social Science Research Council Grant which enabled the author to hire research assistants and carry out the research.

Chapter I

Canadian Foreign Policy and Eastern Europe

Canadian foreign policy is predicated on a number of factors: the geographical position of Canada; a need for a development of trade with other nations; the relationship between Canada and the United States and between Great Britain and Canada; immigration policy and the ethnic composition of the Canadian population; a need for collective security; and the influence of the Soviet Union on East-West relations.

Canada is situated between two important powers, the United States and Russia, who time and again affected Canada's security. Her southern neighbor had exerted and continues to exert significant influence on Canada's economy and culture. The so-called "undefended border" has enabled residents from one country to emigrate, visit one another, and share in sports and cultural activities. In time of war and during the post-World War II period, American and Canadian officials participated in defence plans.

With the emergence of the Soviet Union as a world power, Canada's geographical position became of strategic importance. Such a position emerged as an significant factor during the Cold War period when a conflict between the two super powers would make Canada a "Belgium" of North America. In order to provide some protection from the Soviet Union, Canada entered into the American plan of northern defence named the DEW line, effective against long range bombers but not against missiles.

Foreign policy of any country dovetails with its domestic policy. As far as Canada is concerned this was particularly true with respect to trade and immigration. Canada has had and still has many natural resources which she wishes to sell. Whenever she opened a new mission, she instructed her diplomatic and trade officials to encourage trade with that country. Canada attempted and, indeed, did negotiate Most Favoured Treaties arrangements with most of the countries she recognized.

Although United States had remained and remains Canada's largest trade partner with approximately 70% of Canada's export-import trade going southward, she has had a flourishing trade with Great Britain and the British Commonwealth. To a lesser degree Canada carried on trade with Western European countries and rather minuscule one with Eastern Europe. The reasons for this relatively small export-import trade will be explored in Chapter VI.

Immigration constituted another important element of Canadian foreign policy. Being a vast country, Canada needed settlers to develop her natural resources. Two forces operated with the immigration movement; the "push" force of economic insecurity and persecution influenced many of the immigrants to look for better life; the "pull" force of promises of land, work and good life which attracted immigrants to Canada. Immigration agents advertised in European newspapers benefits Canada was offering to the prospective settlers.

In the First World War and particularly during the Second World War, many Canadians of Slavic origin enlisted in the armed forces. However, the Canadian government wanted to make sure that ethnic groups remained loyal to Canada and to continue nation building. There was a danger that Hungarian, Romanian and Bulgarian Canadians, people whose lands were overrun by Nazi Germany, might prove disloyal to Canada. In 1941 the Canadian government established the Nationalities Branch as a division of the Department of National War Services to oversee the wartime activities of ethnic groups. In December of the same year, Ottawa created an advisory body, the Committee on Co-operation in Canadian Citizenship to assist the Nationalities Branch.[1]

Of some concern were the activities of the Ukrainian-Nationalist organizations. Ukrainian Canadians for decades clamored for the independence of their homeland. This cry for independence received a new impetus when Nazi Germany occupied Ukraine and gave Ukrainian Canadians an impression that Ukraine might enjoy independence after a German victory. The Canadian government was rather worried that the Ukrainian Canadians, the largest of the Slavic ethnic group, might support Germany rather than the allies.

There was another concern. Ukrainian nationalists continued to condemn the Soviet government for depriving Ukraine of its independence in the early post-World War I years. Time and time again Soviet officials protested against the rhetoric of the nationalists. The secretary of state for External Affairs, Norman Robertson, attempted to calm the Soviets by assuring them that Ukrainians, despite their large numbers did not influence the Canadian foreign policy.[2] This appears to be a rather curious remark in the light of concern the Canadian government had about ethnic activities and their nationalistic utterances.

In some respects, Canadian foreign policy was based on a diplomacy of fear;[3] fear of disturbing on-going negotiations; fear of offending the allies; fear of communism; fear of the Soviet Union. This fear was evident even prior to World War II. During the inter-war period, Mackenzie King and R.B. Bennett refused to commit Canada into a path that might disturb the delicate national balance in Canada and that might interfere with on-going negotiations. In response to J.S. Woodsworth, the leader of the C.C.F. Party, who in 1926 raised the issue of foreign policy King replied that "...it would be inadvisable to incur a risk of the kind while the League of Nations in the assembly at Geneva is considering matters of British foreign policy and of great international import."[4] A

---

[1]See N.F. Dreisziger, "The Rise of Bureaucracy for Multiculturalism: The Origins of the Nationalities Branch, 1939-1941," and Bohdan S. Kordan and Lubomyr Y. Luciuk, "A Prescription for Nation-building: Ukrainian Canadians and the Canadian State, 1939-1945", found in Norman Hillmer, Bohdan Kordan, Lubomyr Luciuk, *On Guard for Thee*, Ottawa, 1988.

[2]Bohdan et al., "A Prescription for Nation-building: Ukrainian Canadians and the Canadian State, 1939-1945," *ibid.* p. 92.

[3]Denis Smith, *Diplomacy of Fear, Canada and the Cold War, 1941-1948*, Toronto, 1988.

similar answer was given by Prime Minister Bennett when in reply to Woodsworth's request on Canada's position to the Lytton Report he stated, "it is not desirable to enter into a discussion at this time with respect to a matter of this kind, for it cannot serve the public interest but would be anticipating action that might be taken and therefore is to be deprecated."[5]

One of the consistent fears that influenced Canada's domestic and foreign policies was the fear of communism. To many Canadians, communism was a pervasive cancerous ideology which attacked the basic Canadian institutions of family, church and government. It deprived individuals of the cherished freedoms of press, speech, assembly and worship. Whenever Canadians spoke of communism, they linked it with the Soviet Union where the first experiment of a totalitarian communist state was established. The Communist Party of Canada was closely connected with the Comintern Third International located in Moscow. It was common knowledge that the Communist Party of Canada received and followed the directives given by the Comintern.

Canadians did not wait long to witness a socialist-unionist method of an attempt to achieve a collective agreement. Skillfully led by labour unionists the General Strike paralyzed the city of Winnipeg in 1919. In the minds of many Canadians this Strike was a prelude to the establishment of a Soviet system of government similar to that existing in Russia. During the Depression Years mass demonstrations and riots were staged by the unemployed and disenchanted workers in Winnipeg, Sudbury and Montreal. Again as in the case of the Winnipeg General Strike, radical socialists and communists played a leading role. In 1935 some 900 unemployed workers broke from their relief camp in British Columbia and proceeded under the leadership of Arthur Evans, a communist, to Ottawa; this group increased to 2,000 when it reached Regina. Prime Minister R.B. Bennett frightened by the threat of a massive invasion of radicals ordered the police to stop them from traveling any further than Regina. Violence ensued resulting in the death of two people and in the injury of scores of others.

Ontario reacted vigorously against the radical propaganda and behavior of communists. On August 11, 1931, the Toronto

---

[4]Canada, *House of Commons Debates, March 15, 1926*, p. 1561, Ottawa.
[5]*Ibid.*, November 18, 1932, p. 1368.

city police, aided by the R.C.M.P., raided the Communist Party of Canada headquarters in Toronto and seized communist literature and arrested its leaders. These arrests were made under section 98 of the Criminal Code which forbade the establishment of and the association with any organization that advocated violence to achieve its objective. Seven of the leaders received sentences of five years for conspiring with a foreign power (Russia) to overthrow the existing democratic institutions.

The arrest of the leaders did not eliminate communist activities in Canada. The communists continued to woe the unemployed, disenchanted and marginalized, promising them an utopia of material well-being, as they allegedly claimed, existed in the Soviet Union. From the time Nazi Germany invaded the Soviet Union in 1941 until the end of the war in 1945, the Canadian communists took advantage of the prevailing Canadian sympathetic atmosphere towards the suffering Russian people to spread their propaganda. Canadians appreciated the enormous sacrifices Russians were making in the defence of their motherland. It is no wonder that by 1945 the Communist Party of Canada increased its membership to 18,000 active card-carrying members and an estimated 350,000 communist sympathizers.[6]

The wartime friendship between Canada and the Soviet Union received a jolt when Igor Gouzenko, the Russian cipher clerk at the Soviet Embassy in Ottawa defected in 1946 and revealed to the Canadian authorities the extent of a Soviet spy system operating in Canada during the war years. Some of the members of the Canadian and British civil service, scientists and a member of parliament were implicated in this spy ring.

Prime Minister Mackenzie King was shocked to learn of the espionage. Distraught, he secretly informed the president of the United States and the prime minister of the United Kingdom of the unbelievable series of events in which, according to Gouzenko, the Soviet Union was involved. Upon learning the extent of the espionage, Prime Minister King frightened by the prospect of Moscow's possible counter-attack, attempted to minimize the role of Stalin in the espionage by claiming that he did not believe that the Soviet dictator was aware of the part played by the Soviet Embassy in the

---

[6]Ray Atherton, United States ambassador to Canada, to the Secretary of State, Washington, D.C., January 18, 1945. The National Archives of the United States.

espionage. He wasted little time in establishing a Royal Commission to ascertain the scope and the participants in the spy ring hoping that the Soviet government was not too involved.

Following the findings of the Commission, King's "soft" policy towards communism changed in 1948 when he stated that "there is no menace in the world that is greater (than communism.)[7] But it was left to his successor, Louis St. Laurent to carry on a vigorous campaign against the communists in Canada. Speaking of the Czech *coup* carried out with the aid of the Soviet Union, Prime Minister St. Laurent said: "Those in each free nation who love freedom should draw the clear lesson of the tragedy of Czechoslovakia. That lesson is that it is impossible to co-operate with Communists."[8]

A number of measures were suggested to curb the activities of the Canadian communists. George Drew, the Conservative Party leader urged the government to amend the Criminal Code in order to effectively deal with those who were seeking to undermine Canada's democratic way of life.[9] When he was unable to get very far with his suggested amendment, he urged the government to put into effect the seven recommendations of the Royal Commission — recommendations which the government tacitly approved and which dealt with the communist activities in Canada.[10]

Solon Low, the leader of the Social Credit Party, an adamant anti-communist, suggested that the government should "develop a strong special investigation branch of the Royal Canadian Mounted Police, ...to investigate and report" to the authorities evidences of subversive activities.[11] Like St. Laurent and L.B. Pearson, the secretary of state for External Affairs, M.J. Coldwell, the leader of the C.C.F., believed that the best means of combating communism was to make democracy work.[12]

---

[7]Canada, *Debates of the House of Commons*, 1948, Queen's Printer, Ottawa, p. 2307.

[8]Canada, *Debates of the House of Commons*, 1948, Queen's Printer, Ottawa, p. 2099.

[9]Canada, *Debates of the House of Commons*, 1949, *ibid.* p. 728.

[10]*Ibid.*, p. 2077.

[11]*Ibid.* 1950, p. 78.

[12]*Ibid.*, 1950, pp. 2115, 2135.

In response to the suggestion of the leader of the Conservative Party, the Liberal government argued that the existing laws were sufficient to deal with the subversive communist activities. It was opposed to amending the Criminal Code for a number of reasons. Such an amendment, Pearson argued would stifle the freedom of speech and most importantly would drive the communists underground and prevent the democratic forces to counter openly their propaganda.

Although the Canadian government refused to amend the Criminal Code, it did modify the Immigration Act preventing the entrance into Canada of any professed communist and making it possible to revoke Canadian citizenship of anyone who took an oath of allegiance to a foreign power or who committed acts of treason or sedition. The amendment also provided for deportation of non-Canadian citizens who were disloyal to Canada.[13]

At the same time the Liberal government attempted to unobtrusively monitor Canadians and particularly Canadian communists who traveled to the Soviet Union and to Eastern Europe. Anyone traveling to these areas of Europe were encouraged to inform the department of External Affairs of the purpose for their travel, the duration of the travel and the dates of their departure and their return to Canada. Once in the Soviet Union or in Eastern Europe, the Canadian travelers were urged to report to the Canadian legation or to the United Kingdom legation where no Canadian mission existed.[14]

Ethnic Canadians of Slavic origin applauded the restrictive measures taken by the government to curb the activities of the communists. Some of the Canadians of East European origin felt that the government did not go far enough to curb the influence of the communists. The anti-communist Slavic organizations reminded the government of the suffering their kinsmen/women were enduring in the Soviet Union and in her satellites at the hands of the totalitarian communist regimes.

---

[13]Memorandum on the Amendment to the Canadian Citizenship Act, February 7, 1951, RG 2/18, vol. 139, file C-22-l, National Archives of Canada, hereafter denoted as NAC.

[14]Cabinet Conclusion, "Travel by Canadian Communists," March 8, 1951, R.G. 16, vol. 12, NAC.

During the inter-war period Canada relied on the consensus reached at the League of Nations and on the British diplomatic service. At that period of time the Canadian department of External Affairs was small compared to the foreign office of Great Britain. The Canadian prime minister was also the secretary of state for External Affairs; he was assisted by the under-secretary, by an assistant under-secretary and by a legal adviser. Up to 1939 Canada had only four legations; in London, Washington, Paris and Tokyo. The British legation provided Ottawa with information on various countries of the world including Eastern Europe. The small Canadian foreign service reflected the isolationist policies of the prime ministers and their under-secretaries.

During World War II Canada abandoned its isolationist policy and embarked upon an internationalist one. The one time, nationalist isolationist, Mackenzie King supported the Canadian war effort, even risking the good will of the French Canadians when in 1944 his government established conscription. To enable Canada to carry on effectively Ottawa opened countless legations. Canada became of age.

Fortunately for Canada, a number of gifted and dedicated politicians and diplomats were on the scene ready to serve Canada in the new international arena. Among them were Norman Robertson, L.B. Pearson, Hume Wrong, Escott Reid, A.D.P. Heeney, L.D. Wilgress, John Holmes, R.A MacKay, Robert Ford and Louis St. Laurent. And although Canada continued to receive valuable information from the British foreign office and from the American state department, Canada made its own decision, for the most part, based on her security interests, her position as a middle power and her domestic needs. She used the League of Nations and later the United Nations as "counter-weights" against an over-dependence on Great Britain and the United States.

The new crop of internationalists emphasized the contributions of Canada to the successful prosecution of the war and the maintenance of peace. This approach to foreign policy was known as "functionalism." Canada argued, rather persuasively that, regardless of her small population, she should have representatives on various international committees and organizations because she had contributed, men, material and money. For instance, Canada felt that she should be a member on the executive of the United Nations Relief and Rehabilitation Administration (UNRRA) on the

United Nations Commission on war criminals and on the United Nations Atomic Energy Commission. Soviet Union continued to oppose Canada's membership to these organizations claiming that Great Britain represented all the members of the British Commonwealth, including Canada.[15]

The Bolshevik Revolution and the entrenchment of the communist government in Russia was not welcomed by Canadians who considered the communist regime as Godless and ruthless. The Communist Party of Canada (CPC) who followed the directives of the Kremlin and was singled out as the perpetrator of strikes and social unrest. When Hitler and Stalin signed the Ten Years Non-Aggression Pact on September 23, 1939, the Canadian government banned the CPC and prohibited the shipment of food and material to Russia, fearing that this material could fall into the hands of the Germans. Prime Minister Mackenzie King reacted to the Pact saying that he "never trusted the Russians."[16]

All this changed when Hitler invaded Russia in June, 1941. The ban on the CPC was lifted, war material and food supplies were shipped to Russia channelled through the Mutual Aid Act and the United Nations Relief and Rehabilitation Administration (UNRRA). Prominent public figures, including Mackenzie King, lieutenant governors, chief justice of the Supreme Court of Canada and the archbishop of Quebec came to the support of the beleaguered Russian people.

During the war, strains and tensions appeared between the allies and the Soviet Union. Stalin delayed acknowledging the receipt of food, clothing and war material sent to him by the allies. He clamored for the opening of a Western front in order to relieve his hard pressed forces fighting on the Eastern front. At the Teheran and the Yalta conferences Stalin insisted on the re-drawing of the Polish boundaries and the establishment of friendly governments in each of the East European states. Such demands did not

---

[15]See William McGrath "Canada and the Soviet Union at the United Nations," pp. 84-88 and Donald Page, "Getting to Know the Russians, 1943-1948," in Aloysius Balawyder (ed.), *Canadian-Soviet Relations, 1939-80.*, Toronto, 1981.

[16]W.L.M. King Papers, Diary, August 22, 1939, quoted in J.L. Granatstein "Changing Alliances: Canada and the Soviet Union, 1939-1945," in David Davies (ed.), *Canada and the Soviet Experiment*, Toronto, 1992.

sit well with the allies who recognized the governments-in-exile located in London.

Every attempt was made to keep the Soviet Union in the war by accepting most of her demands. The allies agreed to Stalin's plans for Poland by recognizing the parachuted Soviet government, the Provisional Government of National Unity. Allies also accepted Soviet Union's sphere of influence in Eastern Europe. Communist governments were established in Bulgaria, Romania and Hungary and a coalition-type of government consisting of communists in key positions was formed in Czechoslovakia.

The most knowledgeable Canadian diplomat on the Soviet Union and Eastern Europe was Dana L. Wilgress, the first Canadian ambassador to Moscow. He was sympathetic to the aspirations of the Soviet rulers arguing that the Kremlin wanted security from outside attacks. He showed impatience with the London Poles who insisted on a Poland completely independent of the Soviet Union. Wilgress pointed out that such a Poland would not materialize and therefore the London Poles should learn to cooperate with Stalin.[17]

Much of which the Canadian government knew about the Russian foreign and domestic policies came from the copious correspondence of Wilgress. Since Canada did not have any missions in East European countries, Wilgress was able to glean important information about these states from representatives of other countries particularly from the Czechoslovakian minister.

The revelations of the cipher clerk, Igor Gouzenko, the Soviet domination of Eastern Europe, the violation of agreements and the intransigent position of Moscow towards the settlement of Germany convinced Canadian diplomats, including Wilgress, and the Canadian government that the Soviet Union was not committed to peace; rather she aimed to spread its doctrine not only in Europe but also in Asia and in Africa. In the eyes of most Europeans, Americans and Canadians, the Soviet Union initiated the Cold War. The Communist *coup* in 1948 Czechoslovakia confirmed this belief; if the Soviet Union communists could take control of a relatively democratic country like Czechoslovakia, they mused, she could also take over other countries.

---

[17]Donald Page, "Getting to Know the Russians, 1943-1948" in Aloysius Balawyder (ed.), *Canadian-Soviet Relations, 1939-1980*.

The Czech *coup* galvanized allies' opposition to the Soviet Union. With the encouragement of Canada a coalition was formed called NATO (North Atlantic Treaty Organization) in accordance with Article 51 of the United Nations Charter which permitted the creation of self-protection organizations.[18] Escott Reid, the assistant to the under-secretary of state for External Affairs was the chief architect of NATO. His clear and persuasive arguments won over to his side, Louis St. Laurent, secretary of State for External Affairs, who in turn, had a significant influence on Prime Minister Mackenzie King.[19]

Most of the Cold War was fought in the United Nations where the Soviet delegates vituperated the allies' representatives on international issues. Canada was singled out by Moscow on a number of occasions as a target of Soviet attack and opposition.[20] For instance, the Soviet Union opposed Canada's membership to international organizations; vetoed L.B. Person's candidacy to the position of the secretary general of the United Nations; opposed Canada's peacekeeping role in the Suez and in the Congo on the ground that Canada would only favour Western policies. Canada and the USSR were on the opposite sides on the issue of the width of territorial waters in the discussions on the Law of the Seas and on the admission of the People's Republic of China into the United Nations.

Canada's involvement in the Cold War was in the context of East-West relations. As a member of NATO she provided manpower and materiel to bolster allied forces stationed in Europe. Of all the factors that influenced Canada's relations with Eastern Europe, the policies of the Soviet Union were the most important. One could say that Canada's relations with Eastern Europe were, by in large, determined by Canada's relations with the Soviet Union, for the foreign policies of Soviet Satellites were dictated by the Kremlin.

---

[18]See Escot Reid's monograph, *Time of Fear and Hope,* Toronto, 1977.

[19]J.L. Granatstein, *The Ottawa Men, op.cit.* p. 250.

[20]See William McGrath, "Canada and the Soviet Union at the United Nations," in Aloysius Balawyder (ed.) *Canadian-Soviet Relations, 1939-1980, op.cit.*

Chapter II

Poland:
"Poland is not lost while we are alive"

The Polish resistant spirit is depicted in its motto given above. During its one thousand history Polish people fought valiantly and persistently against overwhelming odds. At times they were successful while at other times they were not. And even while conquered they did not "give up"; they preserved their language, culture and their religion. This was particularly evident during the one hundred and twenty-three years (1795-1918) of occupation by Russia, Prussia and Austria. This spirit is also evident in the fourth partitioning of Poland by the German and Russian forces in September, 1939. During the Second World War Poles endured untold hardships and mistreatment at the hands of the conquerors but refused to abandon their dream of an independent Poland.

There are a number of meaningful connections between Canada and Poland during this period of conflict. Canada declared war on Nazi Germany on September 10, ten days after Hitler invaded Poland. Canadians and Poles fought side by side in the Battles of Britain and of the Atlantic as well as in Italy and in Normandy. To provide a more effective channel of communication, Canada named General Georges Vanier as its minister to the Polish government-in-exile located in London and the Polish government appointed Wiktor

Podoski as the Envoy Extraordinary and Minister Plenipotentiary to Canada.[21] Through these diplomatic channels both countries were able to work more closely in the war effort. On July 11, 1940, Podoski asked and received permission from the Canadian government to store in Ottawa a wireless set, Polish gold and Polish art treasures.[22] Through the same channels, Poland negotiated with Canada in setting up of military training camps. After a series of meetings the Polish and Canadian officials agreed on the financial arrangements and on the logistics of army camps to be in Windsor and Owen Sound. The Polish government hoped that it could build strong armed forces which would eventually help in the liberation of Poland. Two Canadian officers, Lieutenant Colonel A.D. La Pan and Major C.L. Young were to assist in the training young Polish Canadian/Polish and Polish national recruits. Despite a vigorous recruiting campaign only 200 out of the possible 42,000 volunteers responded to the call. Rather unexpectedly Polish authorities found an over-abundance of recruits elsewhere. Some 50,000 Polish citizens were permitted by Moscow to travel to the Middle East where a good number entered the Polish armed forces.

Despite the failure of the proposed Canadian training scheme a bond between the two countries was being cemented. Prime Minister General Wladyslaw Sikorski, after his visit to Ottawa, wrote the following to Prime Minister Mackenzie King: "Our meetings in Ottawa are symbolizing the closer relations which have been established between Poland and Canada and which I am convinced will further develop after the victory is achieved."[23]

And indeed closer relations were established on both civilian and military levels. The Third Polish Division, the First Canadian Corps and the Second Polish Corps carried out joint attacks against the Germans in Italy. In Normandy, the Polish first Armored Division under General Stanislaw Maczek, was integrated into the First Canadian army. One of the most memorable

[21]Secretary of State for External Affairs to the High Commissioner in Great Britain, Department of External Affairs (hereafter noted as DEA): File 26-EC-40, November 20, 1941, National Archives of Canada (hereafter noted as NAC).

[22]Wiktor Podoski to DEA, July 11, 1940, DEA, *ibid.*

[23]Wladyslaw Sikorski to W.L. Mackenzie King, April 3, 1942, W.L. King Papers, M.G. 26, J1, Volume 335, NAC.

battles of the Second World War took place at Falaise where Canadian and Polish forces pinned down the retreating German forces. General Henry Crerar, the commander of the First Canadian Army had this to say about the calibre of the Polish forces: "...in all the fighting of the first Canadian Army during the past three months, the Polish troops have set the finest military standards."[24]

On the home front, 550 Polish engineers and technicians were invited to work in Canadian war industries. These skilled technicians escaped from Poland at the time when German and Soviet forces invaded their country and then travelled through Czechoslovakia, some through Romania and still others through Hungary reaching France. With the fall of France they escaped to England where they were recruited by the Canadian Minister Munitions and Supplies, C.D. Howe to work in airplane industries. A number of Canadian officials including Howe praised the contribution of the Polish engineers to the war effort. L.A. Wright, secretary general of the Engineering Institute of Canada wrote: "Our experience with these [Polish] engineers has been excellent.... The one thing that has made them particularly valuable to us during the war and even now is that they have been specialized in branches of engineering of which we know less then our brethren in Europe."[25]

The sacrifices of the Polish people, including those of the Polish armed forces and the Polish engineers, did not translate into their cherished dreams, the independence of Poland. As the war was nearing its end and the German forces were being pushed back into their own country, it became evident that the Soviet Union had its own designs on the future of Poland. The KGB and the Soviet and German forces eliminated thousands of Polish intellectuals and leaders at Katyn forest and at the Battle of Warsaw, 1944. Stalin wanted a buffer zone consisting of the East European Countries to shield the Soviet Union from a surprise attack from the West. He insisted at the Yalta Conference that the Polish Eastern boundaries were to follow the Curzon line. The Polish govern-

---

[24]H.D.J. Crerar to Stanislaw Maczek, July 29, 1954, Grudzinski Private Archives.

[25]Eryk Rosko, "Polish Engineers in Canada...Their Contribution to the Development of the Country." (A paper presented to the Second Conference on Canadian Slavs, Ottawa, June 9-11, 1962.)

ment-in-exile argued for the former inter-war boundaries which would also include the city of Lwow.[26]

The second contentious issue centred around the recognition of the Provisional government of National Unity. This government emerged from the Lublin Committee, initially formed on July 21, 1944. Seven out 15 members of this Committee were avowed communists indoctrinated in Moscow. On December 31, 1944, the Lublin Committee declared itself the Provisional Government of Poland of National Unity. Five days later, on January 5, 1945, Moscow accorded its recognition to this government. Polish government-in-exile objected to the recognition of the newly created government claiming that the protocol and article three of the Agreement on Mutual Assistance, an Agreement signed by the United States, Great Britain, and the Soviet Union, clearly violated the sovereignty of the Polish state. An official of the Polish government-in-exile criticized the signatories of the Yalta Conference, particularly Churchill and Roosevelt, for allowing the Soviet Union to deprive "the Polish nation of a free will, to decide its own fate, its own form of government and its relations with foreign states."[27]

Although Canada was not a party of the decisions made at the Yalta Conference she was duly informed by the Commonwealth Office of the decisions made by the Big Three. The Canadian prime minister, was frequently urged by the Polish minister to Canada and by the Polish Canadian Congress to support the policies of the Polish government-in-exile.[28]

When it came to the recognition of the Provisional Government of National Unity, the Canadian government followed Great Britain and the United States on the grounds that this recognition was consistent with the Crimean Declaration on Poland and that it would enable Poland to become a charter member of the United

---

[26]W. Babinski to G.J. McIraith, M.P., February 25, 1945, Ethnic Archives, NAC.

[27]W. Babinski, to the secretary of state for External Affairs {hereafter noted as SSEA}, June 29, 1945, Ethnic Archives, NAC.

[28]Memorandum for the Prime Minister, March 9, 1945, R.G. 25, acc. 83-84/ 233(2) Box 26, File 266-4c, NAC: Wladyslaw Babinski, Polish Minister to Canada, to SSEA, June 29, 1945; Polish Canadian Congress to W.L. Mackenzie King, April 11, 1945, Ethnic Archives, NAC.

Nations.[29] In a telegram to the Provisional government Prime Minister King wrote:

> I am pleased to inform you that the Government of Canada welcomes the establishment on June 28, 1945, of the Polish Provisional Government of National Unity and is glad to recognize it as the provisional government of Poland. The Canadian government is therefore prepared to enter into diplomatic relations with the Polish Provisional Government of National Unity and to make arrangements for the exchange of diplomatic representatives in due course.[30]

A day after Canada recognized the Provisional Government of National Unity, the president of the Canadian Polish Congress, which represented 134 Polish organizations asked, rather belatedly, the Canadian prime minister, to refrain from recognizing the newly formed government. Perhaps the president did not know that Prime Minister Mackenzie King had already sent a telegram to Warsaw recognizing the Provisional Government. In his letter the president strongly urged Canada not to follow the footsteps of Great Britain and the United States. He nostalgically reminded the prime minister of the wartime co-operation between the two countries.[31]

The Canadian Polish Congress was also concerned with the type of elections that were to take place in Poland. The under-secretary of state for External Affairs tried to calm the fears of the Congress maintaining that the elections would be held under the close scrutiny of the governments of the United Kingdom and the United States.[32] The fears of the Polish Congress were justified; during the elections of January 1947, bribery, coercion and intimidation were rampant.[33] Polish Peasant Party candidates were prevented from campaigning; many of them were imprisoned on

---

[29]N.A. Robertson, under secretary of state for External Affairs, to J.S.W. Grocholski, July 17, 1945, Ethnic Archives, NAC.

[30]W.L. Mackenzie King to M. Osubka-Morawska, July 5, 1945, M.G.26, J 4, vol. 321, King Papers, NAC.10.

[31]J.S.W. Grocholski, president of the Canadian Polish Congress to W.L. Mackenzie King, July 6, 1945, Ethnic Archives, NAC.

[32]N.A. Robertson, SSEA to J.S.W. Grocholski, July 17, 1945, Ethnic Archives, NAC.

[33]R.F. Leslie, *The History of Poland since 1863,* Cambridge University Press, 1980, p. 294.

trumped up charges. The popular leader of the Party, Stanislaw Mikolajczyk, was threatened with litigation, a threat that would have been carried out had not he escaped to England before his trial. It was not a surprise to have the pro communist Democratic bloc receive 394 seats in the sejm whereas the Peasant Party eked out twenty-eight seats.[34]

As agreed the two governments established diplomatic missions. Dr. Alfred Fiderkiewicz, became the Polish minister to Canada and K.P. Kirkwood, the Canadian chargé d'affaires to Poland. Fiderkiewicz arrived in May and presented his credentials to Prime Minister Mackenzie King on May 31, 1946. He received a cool reception from the members of the Canadian Polish Congress. However, a delegation headed by Wladyslaw Dutkiewicz and T. Lewandowski, both members of the Communist Party of Canada, greeted Fiderkiewicz.[35]

The Canadian chargé d'affaires, K.P. Kirkwood, arrived in Poland on May 7, 1947, a year later than the Polish minister's arrival in Canada. Kirkwood was one of the career diplomats who opened many Canadian missions. In this respect he was a pioneer blazing new paths in Canadian diplomatic history. He opened missions in Japan, New Zealand and Egypt where he worked in rather primitive quarters.

In Poland he operated from a room located in a severely war damaged hotel. In the instructions given by the Department of External Affairs, Kirkwood was mandated to develop friendly relations with Poland, report on the political and economic structures of the country and to represent Canada's interests.[36]

The Polish minister, Fiderkiewicz, received similar instructions from his government. Before departing for Canada, the Polish President, Boleslaw Bierut, mandated that Fiderkiewicz should take immediate steps in having the Polish art treasures returned to Poland. These treasures included the crowning sword, Gutenberg Bible, Chopin manuscripts, and seventeenth century arrases.

The newly arrived Polish minister did not waste any time in carrying out the wishes of his president. He contacted Canadian

[34]*Ibid.*

[35]A. Fiderkiewicz, *Na Placowce w Kanadzie,* Warsaw, 1973, p. 21.

[36]A letter of Instruction from the Department of External Affairs to K.P. Kirkwood, March 12, 1947, DEA files #97605-40, National Archives of Canada.

government officials and the two Polish Art custodians, Jozef Polkowski and August Zaleski who brought this collection to Canada.[37] The latter agreed to co-operate with the minister, whereas the former expressed his allegiance to the Polish government-in-exile rather than to the government in Warsaw. At this point in time the Polish government-in-exile did not wish to return the collection to a government that it felt could not be trusted; it felt that there was a danger that the precious collection could easily be whisked away to Russia to be distributed and mutilated as it happened to some of the Polish collections after the partitionings of Poland in the eighteenth century. The Canadian government promised to be helpful in locating the treasures but pointed out that it neither agreed to preserve the Polish collection nor to return it to Poland; it was up to the two custodians to do so.[38]

Exasperated, Fiderkiewicz sought the help of the Royal Canadian Mounted Police. After an intensive search they found the Polish tapestries in the basement of the Hotel Dieu Convent in Quebec city.[39] The RCMP immediately placed a guard at the entrance to the basement to prevent the disappearance of the collection. In the meantime officials representing the Polish government-in-exile asked permission from Premier Maurice Duplessis to store them in the Quebec Provincial museum. A great friend of the London Poles and an enemy of communism, Duplessis gladly acceded to this request.

The Warsaw Provisional Government of National Unity reserved its strongest words of condemnation for Canada rather than for Quebec. Inspired by the communist Polish Workers Party, the Polish state newspapers, radio, trade unions, university students and some academicians poured out their venom against Ottawa,[40] accusing Canada of being helpless against Quebec. In the Wawel Castle, Krakow, where the arrases used to hang before they

---

[37]For complete account of the detention and the release of the Polish collection, see author's monograph: *The Odyssey of the Polish Treasures* and Chapter IX of his other monograph: *The Maple Leaf and the White Eagle: Canadian-Polish Relations, 1918-1978.*

[38]*Ibid.*

[39]Memorandum, October 28, 1948 837-40C, DEA files, NAC

[40]See author's monograph: *Maple Leaf and the White Eagle,* pp. 198-202.

were shipped abroad to Canada, a multi-lingual sign blamed Canada for stealing this precious collection.

Duplessis also blamed Canada but for a different reason.[41] Never fond of the federal government, the Quebec Premier accused Canada of collaborating with Stalin who, he said, imposed his regime upon the Polish people by force, murder and anti-democratic means. Speaking in the House of Commons on March 4, 1948, Louis St. Laurent, the minister for External Affairs, refuted Duplessis's allegation claiming that Canada never agreed to preserve the Polish treasures nor to return them to Poland; that was the responsibility of the two custodians.[42]

In the spring of 1949, United Nations became the forum for attacks and counter-attacks. On April 25, 1949, J. Katz-Suchy, the Polish UN representative, alleged in the plenary meeting of the General Assembly, that by the very fact that Canada provided storage space for the collection, she hereby acknowledged the treasures to be Polish state property, and was therefore obliged to return them to Poland.[43] The Canadian representative to the UN, General A.G.I. McNaughton, reiterated the Canadian position; Canada never accepted any responsibility for the preservation nor the return of the national relics. He also pointed out that the Polish government could use Canadian courts to prosecute those who unlawfully were detaining the Polish property.[44] The Polish government rejected this suggestion on the grounds that the treasures belonged to the Polish state and not to Canada.

The only hope in this dilemma occurred in May, 1948 when the new Polish minister, Eugeniusz Milnikiel, shipped a small portion of the Polish collection left in the Ottawa Experimental Farm where the tapestries were originally kept.[45] Despite his concerted effort to bring all the treasures back to Poland, he was unable to do so. Frustrated and disappointed, he asked his government to

---

[41]Premier Duplessis reported in the Ottawa *Journal*, March 31, 1948.

[42]Canada, *Debates of the House of Commons*, Ottawa, March 4, 1948.

[43]Allegation of the Polish representative contained in a dispatch A.G.L. McNaughton sent to St. Laurent, April 28, 1949, 837 40C, DEA files, National Archives of Canada.

[44]*Ibid.*

[45]Memorandum on the Polish Art Treasures, September 20, 1948, DEA file #837 40c, NAC.

replace him. This Warsaw did, sending to Ottawa a chargé d'affaires rather than a minister to replace him.

Canada continued to be represented in Poland by a chargé d'affaires. There was even some thought given to the closing of the Polish mission. Some of the members of the department of External Affairs argued that the British embassy could, as it did in the inter-wars period, look after the Canadian interests, and thus save money. Others observed that it would be a mistake to close a mission in Poland when the issue of the Polish art treasures remained unsolved and from where valuable information on the Soviet Union could be gleaned. After carefully examining the pros and cons of the proposal, the department of state for External Affairs decided to keep it open.[46]

The unresolved art treasures issue inflamed other contentious issues. Over and over again the Polish representatives at the United Nations brought to the fore the alleged mistreatment of Polish groups which came to Canada. One of these groups consisted of the 4,500 General Anders ex-servicemen who refused to return to Poland because she was governed by a Soviet imposed regime.[47] Canada agreed to take them in even though she did not have an open door immigration policy. The Warsaw government accused Canada of forcing these servicemen to come to Canada and work on farms under deplorable conditions and for low wages. The Canadian representative at the United Nations refuted these charges.[48]

The most publicized allegation centred around the issue of Canada's admittance of 100 orphaned girls to Canada where they were employed by the Dionne Spinning Mills at St. Georges de Beauce, Quebec. The International Committee for Refugees and the Dionne Spinning Mills Company paid the girls' tickets to Canada. While in Canada they were housed in hostels operated by nuns who provided them opportunities to learn both English and French. Their salaries relatively speaking were competitive.[49]

---

[46]Memorandum for Jules Leger, "Pros and Cons for Maintaining our Mission in Warsaw," November 13, 1950, DEA file #10258-40, NAC.

[47]For a complete account of the admittance of Anders Army into Canada, see Chapter 7 of author's book, *The Maple Leaf and the White Eagle*.

[48]Memorandum for SSEA; file #1025-8049, DEA, NAC.

[49]*Ibid.*

The Polish UN representative, M. Kalinowska, gave her own version regarding these girls. She accused Canada of preventing the repatriation of these girls who in her opinion were mistreated. The Canadian representative at the UN, Senator Cairine Wilson, refuted these charges pointing out that the Polish girls were relatively well-paid, well-treated and given free transportation to the land of their choice.[50]

The most outlandish allegation of mistreatment centred around the issue of Canada's "so-called" kidnapping of 123 children. During the Second World War, the International Refugee Organization (IRO), attempted to find places where young children could be safe and looked after. The Polish children, most of them orphans, were sent to Tanganyka, later to Italy and Germany, places where International Refugee Organization (IRO) had camps. Canada acceded to the IRO's request and accepted them as landed immigrants. The IRO obtained the co-operation of Archbishop of Montreal, Joseph Charbonneau, who asked the nuns to look after them. This they graciously did.

The Polish UN representative used the word "kidnapping" the children, a term refuted by Senator Wilson; she pointed out that it was the IRO who asked the Canadian government whether it could provide suitable housing, food, shelter and care for these children.[51] At no time, she added, was there a thought entertained about any political or financial gain to be derived from such a decision.

Much of the Cold War rhetoric of the Warsaw government was inspired by Stalin and his henchmen. But in 1953 Stalin died. The world awaited with certain amount of trepidation fearing an instability that might result from Party struggles. A care-taker leader, Georgi Malenkov, ear-marked by Stalin, took over as the secretary general of the Communist Party of the Soviet Union. Three years later, in 1956, Nikita Khruschev replaced him. This ebullient, self-assuring extrovert began to create an atmosphere conducive to limited reforms at home and abroad. He stunned them by a carefully orchestrated condemnation of Stalin. His pol-

---

[50]Memorandum regarding an attack on Canada in the UN, December 20, 1949, DEA file #102518-40 DEA, NAC.

[51]Canadian delegate to the UN to L.B. Pearson, November 5, 1949, DEA file #5475-EA-l0 DEA.

icy of "peaceful co-existence" gave a breathing spell to the ever-increasing Cold War tensions initiated by Stalin.

On the international scene Poland continued to follow the Moscow line. The Indo-China Supervisory Commission demonstrated the existence of unresolved East-West tensions. Proposed by Chou-En-lai, a Commission was organized with Poland representing the East Bloc countries; Canada, the Western allies and India, the non-aligned nations.[52] For almost a year, 1954-1955, the Commission carried out its obligations in the spirit of justice. However, the Berlin problem and the Hungarian revolution, 1956, tainted the delegations' reporting. On a number of occasions, the Polish minority report did not agree with the Canadian one. Once the United States became fully involved in Vietnam, both India and Poland, disagreed with Canada in her observations of violations of the 1954 agreement.

On October 2, 1957, Adam Rapacki, the foreign minister of Poland, proposed a plan for the creation of a nuclear-free zone in central Europe. Canada was willing to support this plan provided it led to disarmament of both the Soviet Union and the West. Moscow refused to agree to the bilateral disarmament, thus erasing any hope in this area.[53]

Canada's inability to support the Rapacki Plan did not indicate a total rejection of other types of co-operation. In 1959 Canada supported Poland's candidacy to the Security Council[54] and at the same year Canada joined Poland and Czechoslovakia on the United Nations Disarmament Committee.

Poland experienced domestic relaxation of tensions. When the Stalinist Boleslaw Bierut, died in 1956 the Polish United Workers Party chose Wladyslaw Gomulka as his successor. Gomulka was known for his policy of Polish "road to socialism" — a policy which led to his arrest during the time of Stalin and led to Gomulka's censure by Khruschev.

Once in power he reached a compromise with the Catholic Church permitting some religious freedom and releasing Cardinal

---

[52]Paul Bridle, *Canada and the International Commissions in Indo-China, 1954-72*, Canadian Institute of International Affairs, vol.32, Ottawa, 1973, p.6.

[53]C.H. Southam to the department of External Affairs, January 20, 1960. DEA files. NAC.

[54]*Ibid.*

Stefan Wyszynski from a house arrest. He discontinued the hated collectivization of land started by Bierut, permitted peasants to engage in private farming and enabled artisans and craftsman to own and operate their shops. Thousands of Poles living abroad visited Poland and some Polish citizens visited the West.

The over-all relaxation in Poland engendered by Gomulka's nationalist domestic policy helped to improve Canadian-Polish relations. The London Polish government reacted favorably to the increasing freedoms initiated by the new secretary general. The Canadian Polish Congress, which opposed the return of the Polish art treasures during the time of Stalin now began to revise its position. It carried out a survey of its members and discovered that most of the young Polish Canadians and 85% of the older generation agreed to the return of treasures to Poland.[55] Curator Polkowski also felt that it was time for the treasures to be sent return to the Wawel Castle where they could receive proper care — care which was difficult to provide at the Quebec provincial museum and at the Bank of Montreal.[56]

Support for the return of the Polish collection emerged from other quarters. Witold Malcuzynski, the renowned pianist, wanted the Chopin manuscript returned to Poland by 1960 in time for the celebration of the 150th anniversary of Chopin's birth. During a concert tour of Canada, he discussed his deep wish with Polkowski and with Adam Zurowski, a representative of the Polish government-in-exile.[57]

The Polish Catholic Church also became involved in the solution of the on-going issue. In his four page letter to Cardinal Paul-Emile Leger, Cardinal Stefan Wyszynski, the primate of Poland, argued for the return of the Polish collection, some of which were Church property; he wanted these national relics to be returned in time for the celebration of the millennium of Christianity in Poland. He also pointed out that the Polish youth were being deprived of the educational and communicative value without these treasures. He minimized the fear of these relics falling into

[55]Memorandum on the Polish art treasures, September 12, 1960, 837-40 DEA files, NAC.

[56]Polkowski interviewed by Andrew Manteuffel, correspondent of *Glos Polski*, June 23, 1958.

[57]Author's interview with Polkowski, December 30, 1972.

the hands of the Russians.[58] Cardinal Leger sent a copy of the letter to Premier Duplessis, asking him to help resolve the problem. Despite the request of the Polish primate, Duplessis continued to oppose such a return. However, when he died on September 7, 1959, his successor, Paul Sauve, expressed his willingness to bring the issue to successful solution. Unfortunately, he died suddenly on January 7, 1960, leaving his successors Antonio Barrette and Jean Lesage to carry out his wish.

The ground work for a legal release of the Polish collection was worked out gradually through diplomatic channels. In November 1955, J.W. Holmes of the department of External Affairs, had fruitful discussions with Manfred Lachs, the Polish UN delegate.[59] In December 1956, Holmes also discussed the matter with M. Sieradzki, the newly appointed Polish chargé d'affaires.[60] N.A. Robertson, the Canadian high commissioner to Great Britain, had discussions with Count Edward Raczynski, the former Polish ambassador to Great Britain and strong supporter of the Polish government-in-exile.[61] These informal discussions created an atmosphere of good-will and co-operation.

The government in Warsaw, the Polish government in London and the Canadian government agreed on the procedure to be followed in the release and the return of the Polish collection. As agreed the Polish Warsaw government was represented by two Polish curators, Professors Jerzy Szablowski and Bohdan Marconi. On behalf of their government they signed documents which guaranteed that upon the release of two trunks held in the vaults of the Bank of Montreal and the tapestries at the Quebec provincial Museum, the Polish government would not hold the Bank of Montreal nor the Quebec government responsible for any damages or deterioration.[62] The two trunks arrived in Poland in 1959 and the tapestries in 1961.

---

[58]Wyszynski to Cardinal Paul-Emile Leger, November 6, 1959, Quebec Ministry of Justice Files, Quebec City.

[59]Memorandum, November 181, 1955, 837 40C, DEA files, NAC.

[60]Memorandum, December 17, 1956, *ibid.*

[61]Author's interview with Edward Raczynski, November 9, 1974.

[62]E.A. Royce to J.A. Chapdelaine, August 18, 1955, 837 40C, department of External Affairs, NAC; M. Sieradzki to Quebec government, December 31, 1960, 837 40C, DEA.

The satisfactory solution to the art treasures removed the main obstacle to a more cordial relationship between Canada and Poland. The Canadian government raised in April 29, 1960, the Warsaw mission to an embassy with G.H. Southam named the first Canadian ambassador. The Polish government named Zygfryd Wolniak as its first ambassador to Canada. With the settlement of the agonizing issues affecting these two countries, trade increased, and cultural, scientific, academic and diplomatic exchanges began to develop.

Chapter III

Czechoslovakia:
The Last Bridge Between East & West

Of all East European countries Czechoslovakia was one of the most industrialized countries during the inter-war period. Its diversified economy enabled it to compete well with her neighbors. Perhaps the greatest strength lay in its democratic institutions initiated by the memorable founders, Thomas Masaryk and Edward Benes. Unlike Poland, Czechoslovakia had a relative stable government during the inter-war period. If Czechoslovakia had been bolstered with the allied support rather than be subjected to the Munich betrayal (1938) she could have resisted valiantly Hitler's aggression. Thousands of Czechs and Slovaks including members of the government, fled their country during the Nazi occupation. Some of them came to Canada. The cruel treatment of the people of Czechoslovakia by Hitler and later by Stalin, paralleled somewhat the treatment of Poland by these two totalitarian rulers.

Hitler made Slovakia his puppet and ruled Bohemia and Moravia with an iron hand. Like Poland, Czechoslovakia formed a government-in-exile in London naming Franisek Pavlasek as her minister to Canada. General Georges Vanier was Canada's representative to the allied governments-in-exile including Czechoslovakia.

In 1944 the Red Army pushed the Germans out of Russia and later out of Czechoslovakia and, with the support of the KGB established a Moscow trained nucleus in Prague under the leadership of Klement Gottwald. However, in the election of May 1946, an election which was relatively free from coercion and bribery, much different from the elections held in Poland in January, 1947, the Communists Party won only 38 percent of the seats. However, in this coalition the communist party held important key portfolios; premiership, interior security, agriculture and information. But the majority of ministerial positions were held by non-communists. Jan Masaryk, the grandson of Thomas Masaryk, was the foreign minister, and another non-communist, General Svoboda was named the minister of National Defence. The president of the state was Dr. Edward Benes, one of the founders of the Czechoslovak state.

For two years, 1946 to 1948, Czechoslovakia enjoyed more freedom than any other East European state. Such foreign papers as the London, *Times* and the United States *Newsweek* were sold in Prague. Czech and Slovak non-communist newspapers were published along with the communist ones.[63] Czechoslovak citizens listened to Western broadcasts using their short wave sets.[64] And unlike Poland, Czechoslovakia had relatively little mail censorship.

On the international scene, after World War II, Czechoslovakia did not have serious boundary disputes as was experienced by Poland. Except for the region of Sub-Carpathian Ruthenia, which was eventually given to the Soviet Union, the map of Czechoslovakia remained the same geographically as it was in 1939. Little was said about Czechoslovakia at the Teheran and Yalta conferences except that the Big Three considered it in the Russian sphere of influence. Unlike the ill-feeling generated by the detention of the Polish art treasures, there existed an atmosphere of cordiality between Czechoslovakia and Canada. In 1946, the Czechoslovakian government conferred military honours on eighteen Canadian army and air force officers for their contribution to the liberation of the country. These officers helped train the Czech and Slovak

---

[63]R.M. Macdonell to the secretary of state for External Affairs (hereafter noted as SSEA), August 28, 1947, R.G. 25, acc 83-84/268 Box 313, National Archives of Canada (hereafter noted as NAC).

[64]*Ibid.*

recruits in Canada. The highest honour, that of the White Lion, was awarded to the Canadian commander, H.D.G. Crerar, under whom the Czech and Slovak recruits served.[65] To underscore the prestige attached to this reward, General Dwight Eisenhower, General Montgomery and Marshal Tito, were the three other recipients of this reward.

Upon his return to Canada, Crerar began a campaign for the establishment of a legation in Prague.[66] Since the political, social and economic conditions in Czechoslovakia were relatively good, the department for External Affairs realized the importance of such post; it could serve as a useful bridge between the East and the West. Western ideas could be transmitted to the communist world through this post and a cautious listening post could provide Canada with information about the Soviet bloc. One of the major problems was to find a suitable person for this position. General Crerar declined the offer of the post for personal reasons.[67] Thereupon the department for External Affairs decided to dip into its rather small reserve of seasoned diplomats and chose Ronald M. Macdonnell as its first representative to Prague.[68]

Macdonnell served in various postings prior to the Prague one. He spent a number of years at the embassies in Washington and in Moscow. He also served as the secretary of the Canadian section of the Permanent Joint Board on Defence. His experiences in the capitals of the two super powers provided him with the rather unique opportunity to understand what were the major issues of the Cold War and what were the best means of lessening the tensions between the East and the West.

Macdonnell took up his position in March 1947. His skeleton staff consisted of a second secretary, J.A. McCordick and an air attaché; later an army attaché was added. The physical facilities for this mission were far from being ideal; the members worked

[65]H.D.G. Crerar to SSEA, October 21, 1946, R.G.25, acc 83-84/268, vol. 311, file 37121-40c, Department of External Affairs (hereafter noted as DEA) files, NAC.

[66]Ibid.

[67]Crerar to W.L. Mackenzie King, November 8, 1946, W.L.M. King Papers, M.G. 26 J1, vol. 401.

[68]See F.J. McEvoy, "The Last Bridge Between East and West: Canada's Diplomatic Relations with Czechoslovakia, 1945-48," A paper prepared at the DEA.

out of the Ambassador Hotel where the sitting room served as a chancery.[69]

Macdonnell wasted no time in carrying out the instructions given him by the department of External Affairs. He presented his credentials to Jan Masaryk, the foreign minister, whom he found to be very friendly. Once he became well acquainted with Prague and its immediate environs, he paid a visit to the Bratislava, the capital of Slovakia.[70] While in this city he called on Dr. Jozef Lettrier, the head of the Democratic Slovak Party and the president of the Slovak National Council. He also visited Dr. Gustav Husak, a communist chairman of the Board of Commissioners. Macdonnell was in Bratislava on another mission. He was invited to the opening of the first agricultural exhibition held in this city since the War. In the presence of representatives from the United Kingdom, France, and Austria, the chairman of the exhibition took the opportunity to express his gratitude to Canada for her assistance during the War.

Several weeks later, General Ambrus, who was the Czechoslovakian military attaché in Canada during the War, took the occasion of a glider show in the Moravian-Slovak border to thank Canada, the United Kingdom and the United States for the assistance accorded the Czech and Slovak forces during the war. In the presence of Jack McCordick and the air attaché, Group Captain Cameron, he singled out Canadian officers as having a magnificent spirit displaying first class military discipline in their training of the Czechoslovaks recruits based in Canada.[71]

Towards the end of 1947, there was an indication that the Communist Party of Czechoslovakia was not satisfied with its secondary role. Egged on by the Kremlin, it wanted to replace the present coalition government with a communist one. Stalin insisted that all satellite countries conform to the Moscow hardline policies. All satellites of Moscow, except Czechoslovakia, modelled themselves on that of the Soviet Union. Indicators demonstrated that there was little chance for the Communist Party of

[69]Macdonnell to Pearson, March 24, 1947, R.G.25 DEA file #9390-K-40, vol. 304 acc,84-85/019, NAC.

[70]Ibid.

[71]Macdonnell to SSEA, May 29, 1947, ibid.

Czechoslovakia to gain power in the impending elections; other means had to be taken.

Under a pretext of eliminating high ranking police non-communist officers, who allegedly planted bombs in parcels to be dispatched to government members, the minister of the interior replaced these officers with communist ones. In protest to the autocratic measures taken by the Minister of Interior, twelve members of parliament resigned.

Premier Gottwald denounced the twelve labelling them "reactionary" agents and demanded that president Benes not only accept these resignations but also permit him to name replacements. While Benes was deliberating on some of the options he could follow, the communist leaders of the General Confederation of Labour called a strike as a support for the communist action. In all parts of Czechoslovakia, local authorities were instructed by police to take orders from no one else but from "action committees" appointed by the communist party. Prague headquarters of the National Socialist and Social Democratic parties were occupied by police. By February 25, all vital communication links, all industrial areas and important government buildings were occupied by members of the "action committees." In the atmosphere of such intimidation and control, Benes yielded reluctantly to the proposals of Gottwald.[72]

Macdonnell followed the events very closely and reported them to Ottawa. Along with the facts, he added some of his own observations. He branded the rather impetuous resignation of the twelve members as a mistake in tactics. He argued that the non-communists should have displayed courage and remained in their posts.[73] Two days later, after making this observation, he reported to the secretary of state for External Affairs, that the communists gained a firm control of the government as "the iron curtain has begun to descend."[74] None of the members belonging to the National Socialist Party, the People's Party, and the Slovak Democratic Party were chosen to serve in Gottwald's cabinet.

---

[72] Jozef Korbel, *The Communist Subversion of Czechoslovakia, 1938-1948*, Princeton University Press, 1959. See Chapter II. Note also the dispatch of R.M. Macdonnell to SSEA, February 26, 1948, R.G. 25, acc83-84/268/vol.311, file #7121-40C.

[73] Macdonnell to SSEA, February 24, 1948, DEA file #71 21-40, NAC.

[74] Macdonnell to SSEA, February 26, 1948, *ibid.*

When Prime Minister Mackenzie King was briefed about the events in Czechoslovakia, he was disappointed. "Czechoslovakia at one time a stronghold liberty," he wrote in his diary, "has become a creature of Russian tyranny."[75] Despite his strong disapproval of what he perceived to be a Soviet Russian tactic, he, nevertheless, dissuaded Louis St. Laurent, the then secretary of State for External Affairs from making a statement on the *coup* which, he said, could be interpreted "as an interference in the domestic affairs of Czechoslovakia."[76] With the mysterious death of Jan Masaryk, believed by many to be a murder perpetrated by the police, Mackenzie King became convinced that Russians could not be trusted. "One thing is certain," he noted in his diary, "[Masaryk's death] has proven that there can be no collaboration with communists."[77] The assistant secretary of state for External Affairs, Escott Reid, expressed his shock at the news of the *coup*, for in his opinion, Czechoslovakia had a record of a successful western style of democracy. At the same time he attempted to explain away the Czech *coup* by stating that it was a folly to believe that non-communist parties could participate in coalition governments with the communists and still survive.[78]

Consistent with Mackenzie King's cautious policy, the Canadian government decided not to interfere with the on-going relations between Ottawa and Prague. Instead, Canada supported Czechoslovakia's membership in the International Monetary Fund. A removal from this organization, in the opinion of the under secretary and the secretary of state for External Affairs, would push Czechoslovakia further into the hands of the Russians. Canada also decided not to interfere with the terms of the 1945 Agreement whereby she agreed to provide credit to Czechoslovakia.[79]

However, at the United Nations, Canada joined the United Kingdom and the United States in supporting a Chilean motion to investigate to what extent the Soviet Union was responsible for the

[75]W.L.M. King Diary, in *King Papers*, February 26, 1948, M.G. 26, Jl.NAC.

[76]J.W. Pickersgill & D.F. Foster, *The Mackenzie King Record, IV: 1947-1948*, Toronto, 1970, pp. 164-165.

[77]*Ibid.*, p. 115.

[78]Escott Reid, Memorandum re discussion with the Belgian ambassador, February 27, 1948, DEA, file #7121-40, NAC.

[79]L.B. Pearson to Macdonnell, March 15, 1948, DEA file #50165-40, NAC.

Czech *coup.*[80] Supporters of the motion made statements during the debate. On March 31, 1948, the Canadian delegate, General A.G.L. McNaughton, spoke on behalf of the Canadian delegation. "Events in Czechoslovakia," he stated, "parallel all too closely early developments in other states in Eastern Europe so that they cannot be dismissed as pure coincidence." He ended his presentation by stating that it was difficult "to avoid the conclusion that the Communist Party gained control of Czechoslovakia without the knowledge, approval and some help at least from the Soviet Union."[81] Soviet Union vetoed the Chilean resolution on procedural grounds terminating an opportunity to carry out an investigation by the United Nations.

The secretary of state for External Affairs, Louis St. Laurent, received a tacit permission from his prime minister to bring up the issue of Czech *coup* into the House of Commons. The ice for St. Laurent's intervention was already broken by the Canadian support for the Chilean resolution. St. Laurent believed in Canada's participation in world affairs, a belief shared by L.B. Pearson, the under secretary of state for External Affairs.

On April 29, St. Laurent presented to the House of Commons a lengthy review of the Canadian foreign policy. He referred to the Czech *coup* as "a frightening case history of communist totalitarianism in action" particularly in the light of "the length and the strength of the Czech democratic tradition..." He agreed with his prime minister's comment that the free world could not co-operate with the communists; and he said that democratic forces "must unite their material, their political and their moral resources to resist direct and indirect totalitarian aggression."[82]

Canada maintained its non-intervention policy, not withstanding St. Laurent's reference to a united action. On the one hand, Pearson urged the CBC International Service to desist from doing anything that may be construed as an indication of support for the present Czech government.[83] Instead of criticizing the

[80]George Ignatieff to SSEA, March 18, 1948, DEA file # 50165-40.

[81]Canadian Delegation to the United Nations to SSEA, March 31, 1948, DEA file #5016-40, NAC.

[82]Canada, *House of Commons Debates,* 1948, vol. IV, pp. 3440-l, Ottawa, Ontario.

Czech or Russian governments the CBC IS was directed to show the advantages of the Canadian way of life.[84]

Canada assisted the Czech and Slovak refugees by offering them landed immigrant status. Although there was some concern about finding work for these refugees, most of them being white collar workers,[85] it was argued that they by their skills would assist Canada economically.[86] On July 28, 1948, the cabinet approved an order-in-council permitting the refugees to come to Canada.[87]

On the home front, Czechoslovakia began to experience the full weight of the communist oppression. Freedom of movement, of assembly and of press were curtailed. Visits abroad were eliminated, mail was censored and listening to the short-wave broadcasts from the West was forbidden. Wholesale purging of civil servants, editors of newspapers, teachers, and managers of enterprises by the so-called "action committee" took place.[88] The "iron curtain" had descended, indeed.

Foreign legations began to feel the brunt of the communist oppression. Belgium military attaché and the British third secretary of the British embassy were accused of engaging in espionage and were therefore asked to leave the country. Shortly after these expulsions, Cenek Sovak, a Czechoslovakian clerk translator hired by the Canadian embassy was arrested for alleged espionage. Another local clerk who worked for the Canadian legation was obliged to work in "a labour brigade" for a period of six months making her unavailable for the Canadian legation.[89]

---

[83]Minutes of the Advisory Committee of the CBC International Service, April, 1948, DEA file #9901-5-40, vol. 2208.

[84]Ira Dilworth, the general supervisor of the CBC International, to A.D.P. Heeney, August 12, 1949, R.G. 25, DEA file #9901-AV-40.

[85]Dawson to MacNamara, May 22, 1948, Department of Labour Records, R.G. 27, vol. 287, DEA file 1-26-36.

[86]St. Laurent to Humphrey Mitchell, minister of Labour, June 29, 1948, RG 26, vol. 122, DEA file 3-32-9.

[87]Order in Council, P.C. 3371, July 28, 1948, Privy Council Records.

[88]R.M. Macdonnell to SSEA, February 26, 1948. R.G. 25, acc 83-84/268/vol. 31, DEA file 7121-40c.

[89]A.D.P. Heeney, Memorandum for the Acting Prime Minister, January 9, 1950, R.G. 2, Series 18, vol. 136, file C-17, DEA, and Cabinet Conclusions, R.G. 2 16 vol. 10, January 18, 1950.

The most serious harassment for Canadians was still to come. On January 17, 1950, RCAF Sergeant Danko and air attaché Vanier were accosted by three rough looking men. When these men would not give their identification and continued to obstruct the Canadians a scuffle occurred causing one of the rough men to stumble. Vanier pulled this man by the collar and told him "to get going."[90]

The next day Danko was again confronted at the Canadian legation by a number of other rough looking men. Instead of confronting them, he returned to the legation and was escorted by Macdonnell, Group captain R.A. Cameron and Sergeant Dank to his apartment where non-uniformed policemen were waiting. They did not interfere with the Canadians.[91]

A day later, on January 19, the Czechoslovak ministry of Foreign Affairs delivered a note to the Canadian legation demanding that Danko and Vanier leave the country within twelve hours because of their alleged "abuse of hospitality." Earlier, Danko was accused of obtaining and paying for illegal information related to Czechoslovakia. A thorough in-house investigation of the charges revealed no such espionage.[92]

The Canadian government was distressed by the expulsion of the two Canadians. The under-secretary of state for Department of External Affairs asked the Czechoslovak chargé d'affaires on January 23, 1950, to give his country's explanation for the continued harassment of the members of the Canadian legation and its workers. The under-secretary also wanted the chargé to ascertain whether his government's intention was to obstruct the work of the Canadian government.[93]

When no response came from Prague, the Canadian government decided on retaliatory measures by expelling two members of the Czech legation stationed in Ottawa. On February 1, 1950, the Canadian government asked the Czech government to remove Richard Berhman, a bookkeeper at the legation, and Hugo Beho-

---

[90]Press Release, February 2, 1950, R.G., 2 Series 18, vol.136, file C-17, vol. 1. NAC.

[91]*Ibid.*

[92]*Ibid.*

[93]Cabinet Conclusion, February 11, 1950, R.G.2 series 18, vol.136, file C-17, NAC.

anak, an assistant clerk in the commercial attaché office from Canada within seven days.[94]

It seemed that the Czechoslovak regime did not get the message. They continued to harass legation personnel; this time the wife of the air attaché, Mrs. Doyle, was the target. A couple of non-uniformed policemen, who did not wear customary badges, asked for identification. When she refused to do so they followed her to her apartment. Filled with fear, Mrs. Doyle, who was pregnant at that time, ran the last number of yards to her apartment.[95] The Canadian government issued an official complaint of an unwarranted interference.

The Czechoslovak foreign ministry placed the entire blame on Mrs. Doyle, claiming that she would have been spared police surveillance had she submitted her identification.[96] On the other hand, the Canadian chargé d'affaires argued that the police did not identify themselves to Mrs. Doyle and therefore she did not show her identification.

Because of the inability for the Canadian legation to function normally, there was serious consideration given to the closing of this post along with that in Warsaw. The department of External Affairs studied the pros and cons of such a move. To some of the members of the department, Czechoslovakia seemed to have lost its role of a "bridge" between the communist and the free world; to others it continued to be that "window" to the East and warranted the necessary expenditure entailed in the running of a legation.

J.B.C. Watkins, who served as a chargé d'affaires in Moscow, argued against the closing of the Prague mission. He held that the irritations and frustrations associated with a post in the Soviet Union or in one of her satellites was par for the course; it was normal in any hardship post. For those who found life rather unbearable he suggested a remedy; hop into a car and drive to Vienna, Geneva or Paris for relief.[97]

---

[94]*Ibid.*

[95]Benjamin Rogers, chargé d'affaires, in Prague to SSEA, October 27, 1951, R.G. vol. 3660, DEA file 49-C-13-40.

[96]The ministry of Foreign Affairs to the Canadian Legation in Prague, May 31, 1951, the Canadian chargé d'affaires to SSEA, February 22, 1952, *ibid.*

Canada did not close the Prague mission. Instead the new chargé d'affaires, Benjamin Rogers, decided to cultivate friendly relations with the people of Czechoslovakia. This he did by travelling extensively throughout the country. Wherever he went he found the people friendly and co-operative.[98] Heeding the instructions of the under-secretary of state for External Affairs, Rogers refrained from any words or activities which would annoy the government.[99]

Canada's policy of cultivating more friendly relations with Czechoslovakia began to bear fruit. In 1951, members of the Czechoslovak government attended the Dominion Day celebration. During the same year the chargé d'affaires was invited to meetings of the national assembly, to the opening of music festival and to the anniversary celebrating the liberation of Czechoslovakia.[100]

There were other signs of growing closer relations between Ottawa and Prague. In November 1954 the Czechoslovak government replaced its chargé d'affaires to Canada by a minister. Initially a minister represented Czechoslovakia but the status of the legation in Ottawa was down graded and represented by a chargé. Canada did not upgrade its legation until 1960 when she appointed a minister to Prague; up to this point in time Canada was represented by a chargé. The first Canadian minister to Prague was J.A. McCordick who in June 17, 1960 presented his credentials to the Czechoslovak foreign minister. In his instruction to the new minister the under-secretary mandated him to "facilitate working relationships in the Disarmament Committee" and improve Canada's "bargaining position in bilateral negotiations." In 1962 McCordick was appointed Canada's ambassador to Czechoslovakia.

---

[97]J.B.C. Watkins, A Memorandum for Richie, November 12, 1951, DEA file 11564-40, NAC.

[98]Benjamin Rogers, chargé d'affaires to SSEA, August 1950, R.G.25, acc. 83/84, Box 313, DEA, NAC.

[99]Escott Reid, under-secretary of state for External Affairs, to the Canadian legation in Prague, August 4, 1950. R.G. 25, vol. 3660, DEA files #4900- C-13-40.

[100]Chargé d'affaires Memo, "Treatment of Canadian Legation by Czechoslovakian authorities," to SSEA, June 23, 1952.

Chapter IV

Yugoslavia:
Tito's Separate Road

Out of the three East European countries dealt with in this monograph, Yugoslavia is the least homogenous, consisting of Serbs, Croats, Slovenes, Macedonians, and Montenegrins. It had a population of about ten million people in 1945; Poland being the largest with thirty two million and Czechoslovakia nine million. Yugoslavia was created after the First World War from the former Austria-Hungarian and Turkish Empires.

From 1918 to 1929, it was called the Kingdom of Serbs, Croats and Slovenes. In 1929 its name was changed to Yugoslavia, meaning a country of southern Slavs. Not only languages but traditions and religion of its inhabitants differed; most of the Serbs adhered to the Greek Orthodox religion; many Croats and Slovenes to the Roman Catholic and inhabitants of Macedonia and Bosnia and Herezgovina to the Moslem faith.

The inter-war period was characterized by persistent ethnic strife, government instability and economic chaos. A campaign of acts of terrorism mostly aimed at political leaders was carried out. One of the victims was King Paul I who was assassinated in 1928. In an attempt to curb some of these acts of terrorism, the new king, Paul II, supported right wing governments which curtailed many of the previously cherished democratic freedoms.

Like Czechoslovakia and Poland, Yugoslavia became a victim of Hitler's aggression. The relatively small Yugoslavia armed forces were no match for the powerful mechanized German divisions supported by air power. The country was overrun in a short period of time, but the spirit of defiance inspired resistance movements. One group, the Cetniks under Colonel Mihailovic, and the second, Partisans, under the leadership of Josif Broz (Tito) created for Hitler endless problems, cutting communication lines, blasting railroads and sabotaging factories.

Although the Cetniks and the Partisans had a common objective; namely, to free Yugoslavia of German invaders, there were only sporadic signs of co-operation between the two groups. Tito, a Moscow indoctrinated communist, was an anathema to the Cetniks. A number of attempts at co-operation between the two groups ended in failure; neither of the military leaders wished to be a subordinate.[101]

Mihailovic considered the communists under Tito more dangerous than the Germans under Hitler. On several occasions, Mihailovic agreed to co-operate with the Germans against the Partisans provided that he and his Cetniks receive military aid in return.[102]

When Hitler invaded Yugoslavia in the spring of 1941, King Paul II and his government escaped to London, England where he established a government-in-exile. As in the case of Czechoslovakia and Poland, the Canadian government had General Georges Vanier act as a representative to this exile government.

The British government attempted to monitor the developments in Yugoslavia. From 1941 to 1943, London supported Mihailovic and his followers. But by 1943 it was evident that the Partisans gained control of most of the country. The British government persuaded Paul II to reach a satisfactory compromise with Tito. When Mihailovic refused to do so, Paul II removed him as the head of the armed forces in Yugoslavia and replaced him by Tito. A provisional government headed by premier Ivan Subasic, a

---

[101]Phylis Auty, *Tito*, London, 1970, pp. 185 and 189-91.
[102]*Ibid.* pp. 194, 206, 212.

Croat, was formed. The British showed their approval of the Tito and the provisional government by sending a military mission under Brigadier Fitzroy Maclean.[103]

The provisional government lasted until January 31, 1946, when Tito established a one party regime modeled on that of the Soviet constitution of 1936. All means of production, distribution, security, education and culture were placed under the control of the state and links with the Soviet satellites were formed. Influenced by the Kremlin, Tito refused to take advantage of the Marshall Plan under the pretext that this would make Yugoslavia subordinate to the United States.[104]

In line with the practice of the Soviet satellites, Tito decided to punish those whom he considered had been enemies of the state. Thousands of Cetniks, pro-Royalists and Catholics were arrested, tried, imprisoned or executed for the so-called acts of treason and disloyalty. One of the Yugoslav most wanted man, Colonel Zarza Mihailovic, was arrested in March 1946 and charged with treason. He opted to defend himself without the assistance of a lawyer. Throughout his defence, Mihailovic consistently argued that during the war he did what he thought was right; he attempted to free Yugoslavia of Germans and to bring peace and order to his country. Many appeals of clemency poured in from his supporters both in Yugoslavia and from abroad. Neither his emotional presentation nor the appeals helped to change the verdict; he was declared guilty of treason and executed on July 17, 1946.[105]

The subject of Mihailovic was brought up at the Canadian committee on External Affairs.[106] A deputation of Canadian airmen wanted the Canadian government to exert its influence on behalf of General Mihailovic. In their written presentation they stressed the humanitarian role the General played when he provided Canadian airmen food, shelter and security.

These airmen wanted an opportunity to testify on behalf of Mihailovic. The committee mulled over this request but felt that

---

[103]*Ibid.* p. 220. Major W. Jones, a Canadian was attached to this mission.

[104]*Ibid.*

[105]Duncan Wilson, *Tito's Yugoslavia,* London, 1979.

[106]Minutes of Proceedings of the Standing Committee of External Affairs, department of External Affairs, National Archives, (hereafter noted as NAC), May 30, 1946.

the Yugoslav authorities would not permit such a presentation by foreigners who, would, most likely, consider such a trial completely within their own jurisdiction.[107] Being convinced of the futility of such a presentation, the Canadian government did not do anything about this request.

In 1947 Tito inaugurated a colossal reconstruction programme. The German invasion and the civil war had caused massive destruction of factories, schools, farm lands, roads and bridges. To execute his Five Year Economic Plan, he not only conscripted every able man and women in Yugoslavia but he also asked for volunteers from abroad. This request was communicated through communist newspapers and by national communist parties. Regardless of the political affiliation Yugoslav nationals and ethnics were urged to help in the reconstruction of their "motherland."

A McGill fourth year university student, a landed Yugoslav immigrant, Leon Davicho responded to this appeal by organizing a group to go to Yugoslavia. Davicho was an interesting young man; in 1943 he was accepted by McGill university after he improved his English. Imbued by Marxist philosophy he joined the World Federation of Democratic Youth, sometimes known as the Young Communist League, and became its spokesman.[108]

In his talks to the students, Davicho, promised the students a holiday trip through Europe provided they agreed to work for three weeks on road and bridge reconstruction in Yugoslavia. These students were required to look after the cost of their transportation, but the lodging and food would be provided. Twenty-two young men and women, many of them, non-communists, decided to venture on this trip. They visited London, Paris, Zurich, parts of Poland and Czechoslovakia. In Prague they enjoyed national dances, attended youth concerts and participated in organized athletic events.[109]

---

[107]*Ibid.*

[108]"Yugoslavia," no author is given. National Archives of Canada, Ottawa, R.G.25 acc 83-84/268, vol. 311, file #7121-40c.

[109]"Canadian Beaver Brigade" no author is given but apparently the paper was handed in by Miss Kaye Jackson. From the American Consulate General, Montreal, March 22, 1948; Secretary of State, Washington, D.C., General Service Administration, National Archives & Research Service, 800 Political Record, Washington.

The Canadian group joined forty-five other Canadians from the National Federation of Labour and formed what was known as the Canadian Beaver Brigade.[110] This Brigade along with other groups travelled by train to Yugoslavia. The partying was over for a time as there was a lot of work to do. When they arrived in Yugoslavia it became clear to these young volunteers that the transportation system was in ruins. The main goal of this Brigade was to help build a 150 miles railway from Samoc to Sarajevo. Using picks, shovels and wheel barrows these workers attempted to build earth embankment approaches to bridges. Despite the sincere efforts of the workers from some twenty-one foreign brigades disaster struck them when the bridge built at Belgrade across the Sava River collapsed.[111] Some of the blame was placed on the lack of experienced engineers to guide the workers.

On the other hand, Canadians had reason to rejoice, for they were able to accomplish a lot in a short time. Communist authorities praised their effort and awarded the Beaver Brigade with a Special Distinction Diploma for its effort in rebuilding the railway. A graduate student from McGill School of Architecture was awarded the "Udarnek" badge, a highly esteemed award, for his important contribution to the reconstruction. Six other McGill students received special mention for their work.

Tired but satisfied the members of the Canadian Beaver Brigade boarded the S.S. "Radnik" on their way back to Canada via the United States.[112] Upon their return to Montreal, one of the spokesmen of the Brigade, Norman Nerenberg, told the McGill University students about the work of the Beaver Brigade and praised communist governments of Eastern Europe for their dedication to post-war reconstruction.

A more substantial aid came from another quarter. A communist organization, the Canadian Council of Southern Slavs, solicited volunteers and money to assist in the re-building of Yugoslavia. The response was surprising. Some 350 Yugoslav nationals and Yugoslav Canadians agreed to help in this venture by lending money and "skills and assistance in the reconstruction of

---

[110]*Ibid.*
[111]*Ibid.*
[112]"Yugoslavia" by an unknown author.

the country."[113] Along with the people who set sail on S.S. "Radnik" there was also equipment necessary for this reconstruction.[114]

The Canadian communist party organized in Montreal a banquet on the eve of the departure of the volunteers. Branko Vukelich, acting Yugoslav consul general in Montreal and Edward Vardas, secretary of the Canadian Council of South Slavs, gave brief speeches,[115] extolling the virtues of Tito and his regime.

The Canadian government viewed this venture with certain scepticism, for communism of any stripes was not an ideology it supported. In order to avoid future misunderstanding, the Information Division of the department of External Affairs, made it clear that the Yugoslav nationals could lose their domicile and therefore the right to re-enter Canada, if they made Yugoslavia their permanent home. According to the immigration regulations, these Yugoslavs would be required to formally apply as immigrants to enter Canada. Once accepted by the Immigration department, these Yugoslav would need to wait five years before they could apply for the Canadian citizenship.[116]

The same press release indicated that any Canadian citizens, be they naturalized or born in Canada, would lose their Canadian citizenship if they were absent from Canada for a period of six consecutive years. It warned the Yugoslav volunteers that Canada did not have a treaty with Yugoslavia which provided dual citizenship; therefore according to the Yugoslav law, Canadian-Yugoslav citizens remained Yugoslav citizens unless they obtained a formal release from the government of Yugoslavia.[117]

Canadian government documents do not contain details on the work of the volunteers nor is there any indication how the funds brought to Yugoslavia were used. However, there was a disillusionment with the promised Yugoslav paradise. A number of the volunteers wanted to return to Canada and as expected, encountered difficulties. When the volunteers entered Yugoslavia, their

[113]Roy Atherton, American ambassador to Canada, to the secretary of state, Washington, May 28, 1947. General Services Administration, National Archives, Record Services, 800 Political Record.

[114]*Ibid.* Export permits were granted at this time for $345,918.

[115]*Ibid.*

[116]Press Release, April 30, 1948, Department of External Affairs, DEA library.

[117]*Ibid.*

Canadian passports were taken away from them; some of these passports were returned and some were not. The Canadian legation in Belgrade tried to ascertain as to what happened. At first there appeared some incongruences; 2,000 volunteers made the trip to Yugoslavia and only 870 passports were issued by the Canadian immigration department. After some research the legation discovered that in many cases a single passport was issued to a family regardless of the number in the family. Seven years after the arrival of the volunteers, 650 passports were recovered by the Canadian legation in Belgrade; there were 220 missing.[118]

The Standing Committee on External Affairs was vitally concerned about the missing passports. In one of his moments of frankness, Tito acknowledged that some of the Canadian passports, not necessarily the ones from the volunteers, were passed along to the Soviet agency specialized in altering documents.[119] The assistant under-secretary of state for External Affairs, was unable to verify Tito's statement.

Stalin did not fully trust Tito, even though the Yugoslav leader had direct contacts with the communist party echelons in Moscow. The history of the communist take over of Yugoslavia was different from that experienced in Poland and Czechoslovakia. Yugoslavia was not freed by the Red Army nor was the communist government installed by the KGB. Tito fought and won the right to be the head of the state and to establish his brand of communism. Stalin particularly did not like Tito's independent attitude. On one occasion Stalin denigrated Tito's army claiming it to be inferior to the Bulgarian army which was universally considered as being the weakest one among the satellites.[120] In 1946, Stalin asked Tito to join a Balkan federation, a request which Tito refused.[121]

In 1948 Stalin decided to establish an organization called the "Cominform." With headquarters in Belgrade, this organization, under the direction of the Kremlin, was designed to supervise the economic, social and political activities of the satellites. All East European countries joined this organization except Yugoslavia.

[118]Minutes of the Proceedings and Evidence, Standing Committee on External Affairs, March 26, 1953, DEA library.

[119]Ibid.

[120]Phylis Auty, Tito, A Bibliography, London, 1970, p. 148.

[121]Norman Robertson to SSEA, January 28, 1948, DEA files.

In refusing to join the Cominform, Tito realized the risks he was taking. Yugoslavia would no longer receive assistance from the Soviet Union nor from her satellites; trade between Yugoslavia and the East European countries would cease and there was a possibility of an invasion by the Red Army. Despite all these negative possibilities, Tito took the plunge and defied Stalin — an act very few did in the past and got away with it.

Whereas Tito made an unprecedented step by refusing to follow the Moscow line, he did not immediately tie himself to the western powers. Quite the contrary; he continued to support what became known as "the non-aligned" foreign policy. Along with Egypt, Burma, India, and Egypt,[122] Yugoslavia refrained from joining either the communist or western blocs. This policy fitted in well with that of the allies who did not wish to provoke the Soviet Union by an overt support of Tito.

In 1950 circumstances led to the involvement of the allies. The Cominform economic blockade of Yugoslavia and its crop failure caused by drought made it necessary for Tito to seek western help. The western allies provided food, medical supplies and material for humanitarian and strategic reasons. By so doing the allies strengthened Yugoslavia, making it possible for her to live outside of the Soviet bloc and to resist a Soviet invasion.

The United States and Great Britain responded to Tito's plea for help; the former gave $34.9 million to Yugoslavia to be used for food, and the latter agreed to give £5 million: 2 million sterling for food; 1 million for consumer goods and the remainder 2 million to be used as needed.[123] These were increased in subsequent years.

The Canadian government had difficulty in deciding what it should do. On the one hand, she wanted to follow the United States and the United Kingdom and give a substantial amount of money. On the other hand, Ottawa realized that such help would be criticized by many French Canadians and Roman Catholics who

---

[122]Alvin Z Rubenstien, *Yugoslavia, and the Non-Aligned World*, Princeton, 1970, pp. 43-66.

[123]Memorandum to the Cabinet, November 8, 1950. R.G. 2 Series, 18, vol. 209, file #y-10-1, NAC. This was divided into three parts: a credit of $5.7 million through Export-Import bank; a gift of $12.2 million through E.C.A. and another gift of $15 million under the Mutual Defence Pact.

continued to consider Tito a dedicated communist even though he broke with the Kremlin.

The Canadian Cabinet discussed the topic of relief to Yugoslavia in two of its meetings.[124] The Cabinet agreed that help should be given to the starving people of Yugoslavia and a show of support to Tito's independence from Moscow be demonstrated. However, to minimize the criticism that might come form anti-communist groups in Canada, the economic aid would be channelled through a United Nations organization. There was one direct gift, that of $45,000 worth of cod fish. Through the United Nations International Children's Emergency Fund, Canada gave $210,000 for the purchase of 800 tons of Labrador fish.[125]

The relatively small contribution of Canada did not mean that Ottawa was not anxious to cultivate friendly relations with Belgrade. Both countries agreed in 1950 to raise their missions to the status of embassies. This was five years earlier than Canada's establishment of an embassy in Warsaw. The first Canadian ambassador to Yugoslavia was James Scott MacDonald. The first Yugoslav ambassador to Canada was Dr. Rade Prebicevic; in 1952 he was succeeded by Dr. Rayko Djermanovic. Educated in Yugoslavia and in France and once a member of the Independent Democratic Party, Djermanovic was considered to be open-minded.[126]

On one occasion, however, he showed a lack of discretion. A year after he arrived in Canada he held a press conference in Vancouver.[127] In an answer to a question related to religious freedom in Yugoslavia, Djermanovic said that his country enjoyed religious freedom. As a follow-up, the interviewer questioned the ambassador about the treatment of Cardinal Aloysius Stepinac. The ambassador replied that his government had no choice but to try him for his collaboration with the Nazis during the war. He told the press that Tito gave Stepinac an option to leave the country or be put under house arrest. He chose to remain in the country and, in the

---

[124]Cabinet Conclusions, November 8, 1950 and December 28, 1950 National Archives of Canada, R.G.2, 16, Volume II, Ottawa, Ontario.

[125]*Annual Report for 1951*: department for External Affairs, Queen's Printer, Ottawa, 1952, p. 15.

[126]Relations between Canada and Yugoslavia, R.G.25, acc 83-84/268/Box 332, file#10277-40, NAC.

[127]*Montreal Gazette*, April 25, 1953.

opinion of the ambassador, the pope made matters worse by rewarding him with the title of a cardinal.

Archbishop W.R. Duke of Vancouver took an exception to the ambassadors remarks rejecting his statement that there is complete freedom in Yugoslavia and that Cardinal Stepinac collaborated with the Nazi regime.[128] He was also incensed by the ambassador's insinuation that the pope had no right to make Stepeniac a cardinal. The Catholic weekly, *Ensign*, challenged the propriety of a foreign ambassador to make such a statement.

The Canadian government was embarrassed by the ambassador's impertinent remarks. The under-secretary of state for External Affairs, called in Djermanovic and asked him for his side of the story. The under-secretary admonished the ambassador for making such statements — an admonition he received well promising to avoid such incidents in the future.[129]

Neither the apology of the ambassador nor the rift between the Soviet Union and Yugoslavia eliminated the persistent distrust of Tito and his communist regime. When the question of Tito's possible visit to Canada came up the Cabinet was in a quandary. On the one hand it was politically correct to receive Tito in Canada after his visit to the United States. Such a gesture of friendship could strengthen ties with the West. On the other hand, many of the ethnic groups, French Canadians and Roman Catholics harboured strong feelings against the dictator for his mistreatment of Cardinal Stepinac.[130]

The dilemma was resolved when the United States government decided that the visit was not appropriate at that time; there was too much opposition to Tito making it difficult for the administration to provide a proper welcome and security for the head of state. In the words of the White House press release the visit would "not take place for the time being, because the conditions and atmosphere which have been created in connection with this in the USA have shown that the time for such a visit [was] not ripe."[131]

---

[128]SSEA to the Canadian embassy in Belgrade, May 23, 1953, *op.cit.* file 10277-40.

[129]*Ibid.*

[130]Cabinet Conclusion, Cabinet Papers, January 17, 1957. R.G. 16, vol. 12, NAC.

The cancellation of Tito's visit to the United States and to Canada did not hamper the rapid pace of increasing friendly relations between Ottawa and Belgrade. Canada sent two seasoned and knowledgeable East European diplomats as ambassadors to Yugoslavia; George Ignatieff (1957-58) and Robert Ford (1959-1961) did their utmost to increase trade, encourage cultural exchanges and foster parliamentary visits.

In October 1959, H.F. Davies, the head of the European division of the department of External Affairs visited Belgrade;[132] a visit reciprocated in 1960 by Milos Minc, the prime minister of Serbia. From October 17 to 19 a large Canadian delegation, consisting of members of the Senate under the leadership of Senator Mark Drouin visited Yugoslavia. They had an opportunity of visiting the parliament building and participating in a discussion on the difference between Canadian and Yugoslav systems.[133]

None of these visits engendered controversy; the proposed visit of Koca Popovic, the Yugoslavia foreign minister did. The Canadian Serbian National Committee, an anti-communist group, attempted to dissuade Ottawa from agreeing to his visit pointing out that he collaborated with the Nazis and supported brutal oppression of the Yugoslav people as a member of Tito's administration.[134]

About a week prior to the arrival of Popovic, representatives from the Serbian National Shield Society of Canada met with Prime Minister, John Diefenbaker, and reminded him of what he already knew, that Yugoslavia was not a free country, but a country in which the communists with the aid of "Soviet bayonets" gained power.[135] A telegram from the Serbian League of Canada pleaded with the prime minister to cancel the visit of the foreign minister Popovic, who according to the League, was responsible for the "murder of... many Serbs."[136]

[131]Canadian embassy in Belgrade, to USSEA, February 4, 1957, R.G.25, file #10277-40.

[132]R.A.D. Ford to SSEA, November 10, 1959, ibid.

[133]R.A.D. Ford to SSEA, October 1960, file #10438-13-40, ibid.

[134]Canadian Serbian National Committee to Howard Green, March 29, 1961. file #10277-40, ibid.

[135]Voice of Canadian Serbs, March 3, 1961, Windsor, Ontario, ibid.

The Canadian prime minister's office thanked individuals and groups who sent letters of concern, without promising them that the visit of Popovic would be cancelled. Under close security provided by the RCMP, Popovic visited Ottawa and was invited to the House of Commons. Here he was warmly welcomed by the government and by the opposition parties. On behalf of the government, Howard Green, minister of state for External Affairs lauded Popovic for his courage and his dedication as a commanding officer of the Partisans during the Second World War. The Liberal and the CCF parties spokesmen also expressed their admiration for his effort to free Yugoslavia from the German invaders.

---

[136]Milton Bajcetich, national president of the Serbian League of Canada to John Diefenbaker, n.d., *ibid.*

Chapter V

Immigration to Canada
from Eastern Europe

Eastern European Canadians constitute an important base for Canadian domestic and foreign policies. Their influence varied during the different phases of immigration. The pre-World War I immigrants who came to Canada either to escape the political or social persecution in their homeland or to search for a better standard of life did not exert a significant influence in Canadian politics. Many of them were illiterate and unaware of the events that transpired in Canada or in their homeland. The inter-war period immigrants were more socially and politically sophisticated taking active part in their ethnic organizations and adding their approval or disapproval of the policies of the Canadian government. The post-World War II East European immigrants were for the most part, activists, adamantly anti-communist, fairly well educated and determined to retain their native language and traditions. Directly or indirectly through the members of parliament they elected they exerted considerable pressure on the Canadian government.

There are numerous instances when the ethnic East Europeans took an active role in attempting to influence Canadian foreign policy makers. In 1945 the Canadian Polish Congress urged Prime Minister Mackenzie King to refrain from recognizing the communist-controlled Provisional Government of National Unity. Again the Canadian Polish organization sided with the Polish government-in-exile and dissuaded the Polish Art curator from sending the Art Treasures to Poland. However, when conditions in Poland changed somewhat under Wladyslaw Gomulka, the Polish Canadians agreed to return the Polish collection. In 1948 the Czechoslovak Canadians expressed their anger and frustration when the Czechoslovak communists aided by the KGB took over the control of their motherland. Another active ethnic organization, Hungarian-Canadian Federation put pressure on the federal and provincial government to accept refugees from the 1956 revolution. In 1947 the Serbian National Committee, a strong anti-communist organization, attempted, without success, to have Ottawa cancel the visit of Yugoslav foreign minister, Koca Popovic.

The perception of Eastern Europeans by the Canadian government and by the Anglo-Saxon majority varied. Individuals like Clifford Sifton,[137] the Minister of Interior in the Laurier government argued persuasively for the immigration of East Europeans. In 1896 he began his campaign for immigrants by using attractive advertisements in Western and Eastern Europe. Sifton particularly favoured the immigration of East and Central Europeans, for he became increasingly convinced that these stalwart men and women could build up Canada, develop vacant lands, help construct railroads, extract coal and minerals from the earth and harvest the forests.

Sifton's policy was relatively successful. A decade after Sifton's inauguration of the open policy, the Canadian government fell back to restricting immigration, particularly from Eastern Europe. The new minister of interior, Frank Oliver, led the crusade against the acceptance of people from Eastern Europe. A number of arguments were used to bolster the new trend. Some felt that East Europeans did not fully fit the Canadian Anglo-Saxon fabric since they tended to live in closed communities speaking their native languages and following their own traditions.

---

[137]For useful sources on emigration from Eastern Europe to Canada see the following monographs: J.S. Woodsworth, *Strangers Within Our Gates*, Toronto, 1972; Robert England, *The Central European Immigrants in Canada*, Toronto, 1929; Howard Palmer, *Patterns of Prejudice: A History of Nativism in Alberta*, Toronto, 1982; Donald Avery, *Dangerous Foreigners: European Immigrant Workers and Labour Radicalism in Canada 1896-1932*, 1983.

On the other hand such Western European immigrants as the Germans, the Dutch and the Scandinavians were more easily integrated into the Canadian society; they along with the Anglo-Saxons and the French were considered preferred immigrants. Others argued that East Europeans competed for jobs which the Anglo-Saxon and the French Canadians considered as their domain.

Emigration to Canada*

Table I

	1900-1906	1907-1915
British	703,062	1,852,006
Bulgarians	95	18,086
Czechs & Slovaks	0	1,651
Poles	42,358	67,262
Romanians	2,426	6,371
Ukrainians	269	59,861
Serbs, Croats, Slovenes	5,876	11,933

*This date is based on statistics from the Statistics Section, Department of Citizenship and Immigration, Ottawa.

Understandably, some 2,555,068 out of 2,771,252 immigrants came from Great Britain during the years 1900 to 1915. About 5 per cent of the immigrants came from Eastern Europe. This percentage is higher if one includes the Jews, many of whom came to Canada from Eastern Europe.

Table I indicates that relatively few Bulgarians and Ukrainians immigrated to Canada during the period from 1900-1905. According to statistics there were no Czecho-Slovaks nor Hungarians who immigrated to Canada during the first five years of the 20th century. It is possible that these three nationalities were grouped into the Austrian, German or Russian categories by Statistics Canada. Polish immigrants constituted the largest Slavic group with the Yugoslavs coming second in the 1900-1905 and fourth in the 1906-1915 period.

The Inter-War Years

The war years' immigration was negligible, but it resumed once the veterans were repatriated. Because many of the East Europeans lived in Austro-Hungarian or the Ottoman Empires, they were classified as enemy aliens during the war. Poles, Czechs or Slovaks from the Austro-Hungarian Empire and Slovenes, Croats and Serbs from the Ottoman Empire were placed in the same category as the Germans, Austrians, Hungarians and Turks, the enemies of the allies. After the Bolshevik revolution, immigrants from Russia were also considered undesirable.

Emigrants from Eastern Europe*

Table II

	1920-1925	1926-1930	1931-1939
Bulgarians	578	1,246	155
Czecho-Slovaks	7,628	20,373	5,729
Hungarians	4,100	25,882	3,865
Poles	18,172	33,091	4,057
Romanians	4,903	1,410	437
Ukrainians	3,670	55,361	7,998
Yugoslavs	5,389	15,023	2,834

*Based on statistics from the Statistics Section, Department of Citizenship and Immigration, Ottawa.

This restrictive immigration continued until the early twenties. Led by T.A. Crerar,[138] the leader of the Progressive Party, and supported by a handful of politicians and leading newspapers, an attempt was made to pry open the door to more immigrants from Eastern and Central Europe. Like Sifton, Crerar argued that there was plenty of evidence to show that East Europeans who came to Canada during the period prior to World War I were loyal citizens and assimilated fairly well into the Canadian way of life Many

[138]Canadian Annual Review, 1921, Toronto.

fought side by side with the Anglo-Saxons and French Canadians in World War I.[139] Early in 1923 the Canadian government acted.

The Order-in-Council P.C. 23 of February 15, 1923, admitted to Canada not only farmers, farm workers, but also domestic servants and wives and children of those employed in Canada. This Order-in-Council enabled the urbanized Jews, Czechs and Hungarians to come to Canada in larger numbers. As Table II indicates, the period from 1926-1930 was the time when the largest number East Europeans thus far immigrated to Canada. For the first time in history Polish immigrants were supported by their homeland government in locating suitable lands.[140] For this reason the number of Polish and Ukrainian immigrants, most of whom came from Poland, far outnumbered those from other East European countries. (See Table II.) The number of immigrants from Eastern Europe as well as from other countries decreased measurably during the depression years (1929-1939). (See Table II.)

Economic and political factors played important roles in influencing the emigrants to seek other lands in which to settle. In most of the East European countries land was scarce and life was difficult. The peasants hoped to find a higher standard of living for themselves and their children. In some districts such as Eastern Galicia, both economic and political factors influenced the people to emigrate. The Ukrainians wished to leave Eastern Poland where they felt oppressed and unable to enjoy a good standard of living. Some of the Slovaks in Czechoslovakia felt that preferential treatment was given to the Czechs and not to them; so they wanted to move where they could enjoy equality.

Post World War II Immigration

As in the case of the first World War so in the case of World War II, immigration from Europe and Asia was at a standstill. Wives and children of diplomats sought asylum in Canada during the war. Some 550 Polish engineers and technicians were accepted

---

[139]*Canada, Debates of the House of Commons, 1922*, Kings Printer, Ottawa, pp. 2145-57.

[140]*Ibid.* Chapter I.

into Canada in 1940 where they contributed greatly by their skills to the aircraft industry.[141]

As the war was drawing to an end, thousands upon thousands of East Europeans decided not to return to their homeland. They believed that the Yalta Conference placed their countries in the Soviet Union's sphere of influence. Many of them experienced the ruthlessness of communist regimes in their homeland. They were seeking admittance into western countries. Canada was approached through the East European governments-in-exile, through ethnic organizations and through the British Commonwealth office, to consider the admittance of many of these refugees and displaced persons.

Since Canada did not have an open immigration policy in place she set up a Senate Committee on Immigration and Labour in May 1946. The terms of reference for this committee who began hearing briefs in May 1946 included the following: (a) the desirability of admitting immigrants into Canada; (b) the types of immigrants to be admitted; (c) the availability of desirable immigrants; (d) the facilities, resources and capacity of Canada to absorb, employ and maintain such immigrants and (e) the appropriate terms and conditions for such admission.[142]

The Committee heard briefs presented by A.L. Jolliffe, the director of immigration, the representatives of the two Canadian railways, CNR and CPR, as well as from Cunard the White Star Line; the Canadian Congress of Labour; the right and left wing representatives of such ethnic groups such as the Ukrainians, Poles, Jews, Czechoslovaks, and Finns; and the Canadian National Committee of Refugees.[143] There were also individual briefs presented to the Committee. Among the individuals was Alfred Fiderkiewicz, the Polish minister to Canada. No other East European minister or chargé d'affaires presented briefs to the Committee.

All ethnic groups, except ethnic communists overwhelmingly favoured a considerable liberalization of the immigration policy. Various groups suggested qualifications and conditions for the absorption of these immigrants. Most of them agreed that immi-

---

[141]*Ibid.*, pp. 126-129.

[142]*Proceedings of the Senate Standing Committee on Immigration and Labour,* Queen's Printer, 1946, p. 305.

[143]*Ibid.* pp. 305-306.

gration was necessary for Canada to maintain her place on the international arena and to assist in developing her natural resources. All except some of the communists agreed that Canada, as a Christian nation, ought to do her share in assisting the refugees and displaced persons by finding homes and employment within her borders. At the hearings it was pointed out that such countries as the United States, Great Britain and Australia were taking in large numbers of refugees.[144]

The Committee concluded that not only agricultural but also industrial workers should be admitted. According to one source, Canada had some 27,000,000 acres of unused land, which could be broken up into some 150,000 to 160,000 farms.[145] This did not include lands owned by the Canadian Pacific Railways and the Hudson Bay Company. There was also a demand for individuals with mechanical or technical skills.

Two Canadian railways, CNR and CPR, promised to assist the immigrants in every way possible. The Committee also acknowledged the role of the railways in promoting new industries, tourist traffic and foreign trade. It observed that the two Canadian railways consistently co-operated with such ocean lines as the Cunard, the White Star and Donaldson Atlantic lines in bringing immigrants to Canada.

The Senate Standing Committee[146] was informed that there were many sources of potential immigrants. The Canadian Polish congress pointed out that there were some 200,000 Poles in Europe who refused to return to Poland and were seeking admission into western countries including Canada. Approximately 60 percent were farmers by profession and the remaining 40 percent possessed some mechanical skills. The Committee was also informed that there were thousands of other displaced persons, including Ukrainains, Lithuanians, Latvians and Czechoslovaks who wanted to emigrate to Canada.

After serious deliberation the Committee made the following recommendations:[147]

---

[144]*Ibid.* pp. 314-315.
[145]*Ibid.*, p. 307.
[146]*Ibid.*
[147]*Ibid.*, pp. 316-317.

(i) that the government make a public announcement of its policy to admit both agricultural and industrial workers; (ii) that the number to be admitted was to be governed by Canada's capacity to absorb the immigrants, and by the availability of overseas transportation; (iii) that the Immigration Act be revised to provide for the funding and selection of immigrants of the most desirable types and for their supervision and their assistance. These recommendations were further supported by the report of Allon Peebles, director of research and statistics in the federal department of Labour and of Alex Skelton, director general of economic research of the department of Reconstruction and Supply.[148]

On July 15, 1947, the report of the Senate Standing Committee, assisted by the observations of Peebles and Skelton, was adopted by the Senate. The Canadian government attempted to implement the recommendations of the Senate standing Committee.[149]

Canada's Reaction to Refugees and Displaced Persons

Frequently the terms "refugees" and "displaced persons" are used interchangeably; however, there is a distinction between these two terms. Refugees were citizens or residents of Axis countries who refused to accept their governments, be it German, Italian or Japanese. Displaced persons, on the other hand, opted to leave their country rather than face the probability of forced labour, deprivation of the right to state employment and services and in some cases, imprisonment.

In 1939, over 300 Czech families and about 100 single men from the so-called Sudeten areas in Czechoslovakia were admitted into Canada. With the fall of France, Belgium and Netherlands in 1940, more were admitted as refugees. In 1941-43, 550 Polish technicians and engineers were invited by the Canadian government to work in the aircraft industry.

---

[148]Nathaniel Constantine Allyn, "European Immigration into Canada," (1946-1951), Ph.D. dissertation, Stanford University, 1953, pp. 105-109.

[149]Statement of W.E. Harris, "Implementation of New Immigration Regulations, Order-in-Council, P.C., 1856, 1950, #2. Department of Immigration.

While fully sympathetic with these unfortunate people, Canada, nevertheless, exercised caution in admitting them. Some of this caution stemmed from political reasons, some from security reasons and still others from economic considerations. Quebec members of parliament were very conscious of the delicate balance between the English-speaking and the French-speaking Canadians. An acceptance of a large number of refugees by provinces other than Quebec, would according to these members, prove damaging to the existing stability and harmony of the two founding peoples.

Despite the horrors expressed by Canadians at the mistreatment of people, particularly of the Jews by Nazi Germany, there lingered in the hearts of many Canadian officials anti-semitic feelings. There was also a fear that somehow a few Nazi collaborators might slip in as bone fide immigrants. The labour unions harboured the scepter that the refugees would replace Canadian workers on one hand, and be themselves exploited by the Canadian employers on the other. The Canadian government continued to bring up the subject of the lack of assimilation of East Europeans into the Canadian fabric.[150]

Even with the amendment of the Immigration Act, Canada remained unprepared to handle the enormous number of refugees. The domestic Inter-Departmental Committee and the Inter-Governmental Committee operating from London, England, were swamped with requests for admittance to Canada. In 1946 the United Nations General Assembly established a Committee on Refugees, a committee in which Canada took a role as a peacemaker between the Soviet union and the West. Canada supported the generally accepted view of making any repatriation of refugees voluntary, and disagreed with the Russian policy of forcing such nationals as Ukrainians to return to Ukraine.

The United Nations Committee was replaced by the United Nations International Refugee Organization (IRO). Canada became an active member of International Refugee Organization (IRO), ever attempting to bridge the East-West chasm for the sake of suffering refugees and displaced persons. As a member of the

[150]John W. Holmes, *Canada and the Search for World Order, 1943-1957*, vol. I, Toronto, 1979, pp. 96-98. See also Irving Abella and H. Troper, *None is Too Many: Canada and the Jews of Europe, 1933-48*, and Gerald Dirks, *Canada's Refugee Policy*, Montreal, 1977.

International Refugee Organization (IRO), Canada played a prominent role in widening the immigration quotas. Canada enlarged its quota from 20,000 refugees admitted in 1947 to 40,000 in 1949.[151] All in all, Canada accepted 123,479 refugees during the lifetime of the International Refugee Organization (IRO). This figure is commendable when compared and contrasted with countries having larger populations. Counting those who came through other agencies besides the International Refugee Organization (IRO) Canada accepted 300,000 refugees during the post-World War period.[152]

A number of motives inspired Canada to accept refugees generously and to assist them. Christian and humanitarian motives were very important. But there were other reasons as well. Each country wanted to get the best qualified, healthiest, the most intelligent immigrants they could obtain. As a whole, most of the countries succeeded in getting those who in time contributed much to the intellectual, economic and cultural life of their nation.

Anders Army Veterans

We see a mixture of motives operating in the admission of veterans of General Anders Second Polish Army. Although there was a genuine admiration for the contribution of the Poles in the Second World War, admiration was not strong enough a factor in influencing the Canadian public to admit some 4,500 Polish veterans into Canada. In order to avoid undue criticism of accepting these veterans before all the Canadian war veterans returned to Canada and before they were placed in gainful employment, Ottawa had to find other reasons for admitting the Poles.

The Canadian government was bombarded by a number of serious requests to admit the veterans of Anders Army into Canada. Former Polish consul general, Wiktor Podoski, the United Polish Relief Fund, the Canadian Legion, the Canadian Polish Congress and the United Kingdom made urgent appeals to

---

[151]John W. Holmes, *Canada and the Search for World Order, 1943-1957*, pp. 98-99.

[152]*Ibid.* p. 100. See also Freda Hawkins, *Canada and Immigration: Public Policy and Public Concern*, Montreal, 1972, p. 1.

Ottawa.[153] By far the most persuasive came from the United Kingdom government which demonstrated, on the one hand, the desirability of absorbing these qualified veterans, and on the other hand, the inability of the British government to cope with the influx of refugees.

The Canadian cabinet carefully studied the requests, and in the absence of a refugee policy, sought desperately to find a solution to the dilemma. After considering various alternatives, one appeared to be most plausible. Canada could admit the veterans as a replacement for the 4,000 German prisoners of war who worked on farms until 1946 and now were being repatriated. Thereupon, the Canadian cabinet agreed by an Order-in-Council, PC. 3112, to admit some 4,500 unmarried Polish veterans. The selected ones had to meet the usual immigration requirements; namely, moral, physical and occupational suitability. They also had to agree to work on farms for two years before applying for landed immigrant status. The British government was to bear the cost of transporting the veterans across the Atlantic whereas the Canadian government agreed to transport them within Canada, to provide them with necessary clothing and to place them on farms.[154]

It was decided to select the veterans from those present in Italy and if there were not enough qualified veterans there, to get the rest from the United Kingdom. Security screening was carried out by the RCMP, while the representatives of the departments of Immigration and Labour tested the prospective immigrants with respect to agricultural knowledge, their mental and physical health and their adaptability. Some 2,876 veterans were selected in Italy and 1,624 in the United Kingdom.[155]

Displaced Persons Enter Canada, 1947-51[156]

Table III

Poles	36,549	Jews	15,555	Estonians	8,920

[153]For full details on the admission of the Anders army ex-servicemen see Aloysius Balawyder, *The Maple Leaf and the White Eagle: Canadian-Polish Relations, 1918-1978*, Toronto, 1983.

[154]*Ibid.*, 139-40.

[155]*Ibid.*, p. 146.

Table III

Ukrainians	25,858	Latvians	9,820	Yugoslavs	8,440
Germans	18,411	Lithuanians	9,454	Czechoslovaks	5,074

Table III demonstrated that Poles constituted the largest displaced persons group. It is reasonable to assume that this figure is even larger when one includes many of the Polish Jews and Ukrainians from Eastern Galicia.

Refugees from Czechoslovakia

There was a sincere sympathy for the Czechoslovak people after the 1948 *coup*. A Canadian representative of the International Refugee Organization (IRO) pointed out that there were some 10,000 Czechoslovak refugees in the United States zone of occupation and some 300 Czechoslovak refugees in the British zone.[157] According to this source most of the refugees were clerical workers and government officials.[158]

A Canadian inter-departmental committee consisting of representatives from departments of Immigration, External Affairs and Labour discussed the whole aspect of the Czechoslovak refugees.[159] The Labour department representative pointed out the difficulty of providing white-collar refugees with work. As in the case of General Anders army veterans, so in the case of the Czecho-Slovaks, only those who wished to work on farms or to work as domestics could be gainfully employed. While acknowledging the argument of the Labour department representatives as one point of view, the representative of the department of External Affairs pointed out that there were other factors involved in accepting this

---

[156]"Immigration to Canada showing Displaced Persons Admitted by Ethnic Origin", Calendar Years, 1947-51, 1952, Department of Citizenship and Immigration, Ottawa.

[157]From the PCIRO, Geneva to Secretary of State of External Affairs (hereafter referred to as SSEA), May 14, 1948, RG 27, vol. 287, file 1-26-36, PAC.

[158]*Ibid.*

[159]W.W. Dawson, Department of Labour, to A. MacNamara, May 22, 1948, *ibid.*

group of refugees. He contended that the Czechoslovaks should be given preferential treatment since they suffered greatly at the hands of Hitler and were now suffering at the hands of the communists.[160]

Another meeting of the representatives of Labour, Immigration and External Affairs was held. The representatives decided that 1,000 Czechoslovak refugees should be admitted to Canada and that a national committee for resettlement of political refugees be formed. The committee was to be headed by either General H. Crerar or by Phillippe Blais. The purpose of this committee was to arouse national conscience as to its corporate and individual responsibility in such a humanitarian work, to obtain promises of practical assistance in the resettlement of refugees in Canada and to raise funds to transport and resettle them.[161]

Although the plan to establish a committee was shelved, the Labour department continued to doubt the arguments of the External Affairs department for admitting the urbanized Czechoslovaks. The secretary of state for External Affairs, Louis St. Laurent, wrote a letter to Humphrey Mitchell, minister of Labour, supporting the policy of his department officials. He argued that, although many Czechoslovaks are not agriculturists, they would contribute much to Canada by their "great intelligence, initiative and ability." He raised the possibility that these "free men" who were fighting against communism might be shining examples to other peoples of Eastern Europe.[162]

Evidently St. Laurent's letter did help to expedite the emigration of the Czechoslovak refugees. An order-in-council permitted the Czechoslovak agriculturists and blue-collar workers to come to Canada. Out of 1,304 admitted under this order-in-council, only 200 were farm labourers; the remainder were miners, hydro-workers and domestic workers.[163]

Refugees from Czechoslovakia did get preferential treatment. Unlike the Anders army veterans, the Czechoslovaks did not have to spend two years working on farms; security clearance was

---

[160]"Possible Movement of Czech Democratic Refugees to Canada," n.d., *ibid.*

[161]*Ibid.*

[162]Louis St. Laurent to Humphrey Mitchell, June 29, 1948, *ibid.*

[163]A. McNamara to W.P. Black, Canadian Government Immigration Mission, Germany, February 26, 1949, *ibid.*

waived in many instances, particularly if the individuals were recommended by the former Czechoslovak diplomat, Milos
Nemec.[164]

The Hungarian Refugees, 1956

The genuine evidence of Canada's potential generosity came
with the gradual acceptance of Hungarian refugees. For the first
time in Canadian history did we witness such a widespread reaction to a communist revolt as in the Hungarian uprising of 1956.
Men and women of every walk of life, and political persuasion
expressed sympathy for the Hungarians. Fortunately, Canada had
internationally-minded politicians and diplomats at this period of
time. The team of St. Laurent as the prime minister and L.B. Pearson as the secretary of state for External Affairs, assisted by such
intelligent and forward-looking diplomats as Hume Wrong, Escott
Reid, Norman Robertson, D.L. Wilgress and John W. Holmes,
made the "improbable," "possible." One politician who worked
diligently to accomplish this "humanitarian dream" was Jack Pickersgill, Minister of Immigration.

Since Canada did not have a legation in Hungary, she had to
rely on other sources for information; the British embassy continued to inform Canada through the Commonwealth Office. The
American embassy was also helpful. But, by mere coincidence, A.F.
Hart, Canadian chargé d'affaires in Belgrade, and his wife happened to be travelling across Hungary to Prague during the early
stages of revolution. Marooned on Margaret Island, which is
located between Buda and Pest, they were able to observe personally the attempt of Hungarians to gain freedom and to witness the
brutality of Russian suppression.[165] Hart's account gave another
view of the revolt.

---

[164]*Ibid.*
[165]A.F. Hart, "Eye Witness Story from Hungary", *External Affairs*, vol. 8, November 1956, pp. 339-345.

Initial Response of Canada

The Hungarian revolt was less than a month old when the Canadian government decided to give $100,000 to the Canadian Red Cross for the relief of Hungarian refugees. Soon after the first donation, Canada offered another $100,000 to the United Nations High Commissioner for Refugees to be used for the same purpose.[166] On the occasion of the opening of the special session of Canadian Parliament dealing with the subject of the Hungarian revolt, Canada added $800,000 to the already donated sum of $200,000. The last donation was divided between the Red Cross and the United Nations High Commissioner for Refugees.[167]

The minister of External Affairs, L.B. Pearson, decided to expose the immensity of the Hungarian tragedy at public forums outside the House of Commons. On November 4[168] and again on November 19,[169] L.B. Pearson, secretary of state for External Affairs, participated in the debate in the United Nations. In his opinion, the Soviet Union betrayed the students and workers. At the same time he dismissed any parallel between the situation in the Middle East where Great Britain and France invaded Egypt and the revolt in Hungary. He referred to the United Nations Emergency Force, for whose formation he was responsible; then he rhetorically posed the question whether a similar United Nations force could be useful in Hungary. In his November 19 statement, Pearson suggested a three-man team to investigate and report on the events that transpired and were transpiring in Hungary. He also referred to the United Nations resolutions which called for the withdrawal of Soviet forces from Hungary and for a large scale relief program to assist the Hungarian people.[170] All the

[166]"Canadian Citizenship Act," Cabinet Conclusion, RG 2 116, vol. 14, NAC.

[167]Jules Leger, the Under Secretary of State for External Affairs, to Laval Fortier, November 29, 1956, Department of External Affairs, Ottawa.

[168]Statement of L.B. Pearson in the General Assembly of the United Nations, November 4, 1956, *Statements and Speeches*, Information Division, Department of External Affairs, Ottawa.

[169]Statement of L.B. Pearson in the General Assembly of the United Nations, November 19, 1956, *ibid.*

[170]*Ibid.*

proposed resolutions were passed in the General Assembly with considerable margins.

On November 13, 1956,[171] Prime Minister Louis St. Laurent wrote a letter to Premier N.A. Bulganin, expressing on behalf of his government and the Canadian people, the horror the Canadian people felt "at the suffering of the Hungarian people as a result of their efforts to obtain freedom," and their own type of government. Attempting to be objective, St. Laurent begged the Soviet premier "in the name of humanity" to use his influence "to alleviate the sufferings of the Hungarian people and to permit competent international agencies" to help the needy and the sick.

In his letter of November 24, the Soviet premier,[172] referred to the letter of the Canadian prime minister and to the statements of Canadian officials, terming them as "one-sided, tendentious and unobjective information." He wished to correct the misconceptions of the prime minister and the Canadian officials by stating that the revolution was initiated by reactionary forces with outside aid, who attempted to overthrow the people's democratic regime. He then went on to say that the "patriotic forces" defended people's democracy by asking for the help of the Soviet troops.

The Soviet contention, as depicted by Premier Bulganin, was thoroughly refuted by a special committee set up by the United Nation.[173] Although the three-man committee was not permitted to carry out the investigation in Hungary, the committee did gain valuable information on the Hungarian revolution through interviews of Hungarian refugees admitted into Canada, and through other sources. The report of this committee[174] indicated that the students, workers and soldiers rose against the corrupt and foreign-dominated regime. The movement towards freedom and independence was squelched by the Soviet Union, which on

---

[171]Louis St. Laurent to N.A. Bulganin, November 13, 1956, *Statement & Speeches*, November 26, 1956.

[172]N.A. Bulganin to Louis St. Laurent, November 24, 1956, *ibid*.

[173]The committee consisted of Honourable Anderson of Denmark, chairman, Ambassador Shann of Australia, Ambassador Gunewardene of Ceylon, Ambassador Slim of Tunisia and Ambassador Fabregot of Uruguay.

[174]Statement of Dr. R.A. MacKay, Canada's permanent representative to the United Nations, made in the General Assembly, September 12, 1958, *Statements and Speeches*, Information Division of the Department of External Affairs, Ottawa.

November 3 arrested the Hungarian negotiators and carried out a brutal attack on the common people of Hungary.

Canada's Hungarian Refugee Policy Criticized

Canadian newspapers and members of the opposition argued that Canada did not do enough to assist the refugees. Of the newspapers, the Toronto *Globe and Mail* (November 12, 1956) was most critical of Canada's inactivity. In its editorial this newspaper contended that the financial aid given to the Hungarian refugees was inadequate. What the refugees needed, the Toronto paper argued, was warmth and love rather than a cold and calculating attitude displayed by the officials of the Immigration Department who continued to require the Hungarians refugees to be in good health, have sufficient training in a profession or a job and have an assurance that relatives or responsible persons or organizations would assist them if they could not do this themselves. The Toronto *Telegram* (November 12, 1956) supported the views of the *Globe and Mail*, noting that the United States had similar regulations regarding security checks and sponsors but had waived these for humanitarian sake. The *Winnipeg Free Press* suggested that the minister of Immigration, Jack Pickersgill, "quit his double-talk and let the Hungarian refugees know that this country is prepared to do more than offer words of sympathy."

Was the criticism of the Canadian refugee policy accurate as portrayed by some Canadian newspapers? Such countries as the United States, Australia, and New Zealand agreed to accept about 26,000 Hungarian refugees; France placed no quota on refugees entering her borders; Israel too placed no limits on Jewish refugees entering Israel.[175] Whereas countries promised to accept refugees, Canada continued to walk a cautious line, insisting that sponsors assist the refugee financially if in need and take the responsibility of looking after sick refugees.

---

[175]R.A.D. Ford to the under-secretary of state for External Affairs (hereafter referred to as USSEA), November 14, 1956, file #5475-EA-4-40, Department of External Affairs. The following countries agreed to accept the given number of Hungarian refugees: Argentina 3,000 children, Australia 3,000; Belgium 4,000; France no limit; Netherlands 1,000; New Zealand 500; Israel no limit; Sweden 1,000; Switzerland 2,000; United Kingdom 2,500; United States 5,000; Germany 3,000; Italy 2,000.

A number of forces began to stir up the immigration minister to immediate action. No doubt the newspaper editorials aroused public opinion and awakened a latent sympathy for the suffering refugees. The Hungarian-Canadian Federation (HCF), focused public attention on the events in Hungary by its demonstrations, petitions and its representations.[176] The Hungarian-Canadian Federation despatched a delegation to Ottawa to keep the issue ever before the eyes of parliament. At the same time an urgent request was sent by this organization to the United Nations General Assembly seeking its assistance.

Canada Opens Her Doors to the Hungarian Refugees

On November 9, 1956, Pearson wrote to Pickersgill, pointing out that domestic and International situations made it imperative for Canada to demonstrate her unselfish concern for the plight of the Hungarian refugees.[177] The domestic situation he was referring to was the pending federal election: the international situation was the growing aggressiveness of the Soviet Union. Pearson suggested that the general Canadian regulations on health and job requirements should be waved aside.

Pickersgill was glad to receive such a note from Pearson. He too believed that Canada should do more and faster to help the refugees; however, the regulations of the department of Citizenship and Immigration made it difficult for his "dream" to come true. Pickersgill was convinced that if Canada and other countries did not relieve the Austrian government by accepting some of the refugees, they would be forced to return to Hungary.[178] If this happened, mused the minister of citizenship and immigration, the Russians would point to the callousness of the West. With the support of his cabinet colleagues, Pickersgill lost no time in visiting Bonn, The Hague, Brussels, Paris and London where he tried to negotiate deals with the governments to house during the winter the refugees destined for Canada during the winter.

---

[176]N.F. Dreisziger (ed) *Struggle and Hope: The Hungarian-Canadian Experience,* McClelland and Stewart Ltd., 1982, pp. 203-205.

[177]L.B. Pearson to Jack W. Pickersgill, November 9, 1956, file #5475-EA-4-40, Department of External Affairs, Ottawa.

[178]Aloysius Balawyder's interview with Jack Pickersgill, May 23, 1984.

On a different level, Pickersgill persuaded the cabinet to make a number of changes to the immigration regulations. For instance, the cabinet agreed to waive the usual form of medical examination and to use chartered aircraft to bring the refugees to Canada.[179] It was felt that a minimum medical examination would be given in Europe, while X-ray and other examinations would be carried out in Canada. Both the Trans-Canada airlines and the Canadian Pacific Airlines agreed to fly extra flights to carry the refugees to Canada. At the insistence of Pickersgill, a special session of the 22nd parliament was summoned.[180] At this session Pickersgill gave the House the government's plan to assist the refugees. Then he pleaded for continuous support from all parties, provinces, organizations and individuals.

Cooperation of Provinces

Provinces responded positively to the appeal of the minister of citizenship and immigration. Ontario was the first to offer assistance to the refugees. However, it was Saskatchewan's plan that became a model for other provinces to follow.[181] Saskatchewan established administrative centres where refugees were housed and fed. Every refugee was paid three dollars per day. The federal government paid the transportation costs to these centres and from these centres to places of employment. Saskatchewan agreed to take X-rays and vaccinate the refugees at her own expense. For the first year, the federal government agreed to pay for most of the expenses involving sustenance and the Saskatchewan government agreed to take care of the refugees thereafter.[182] This Saskatchewan plan was accepted by British Columbia and Ontario. The other six provinces agreed to accept the refugees after they were granted a permanent residence status and after they had met the usual immigration requirements.

---

[179]"Hungarian Refugees," Cabinet conclusion, November, 23, 1956, RG 2/16, vol. 14, NAC.

[180]Jack Pickergsill's statement in the House of Commons, November 28, 1956, *Statements and Speeches*, Information Division, Department of External Affairs.

[181]"Hungarian Refugees", Cabinet Conclusion, December 5, 1956, Privy Council Office, Management Branch, Ottawa.

[182]"Hungarian Refugees", Cabinet Conclusion, December 19, 1956, *ibid*.

A Cup of Kindness Without Measure

It seems as if Canada wanted to compensate for the tardiness in accepting the Hungarian refugees with "measureless" hospitality. Before the first contingent of refugees left the Austrian camp at Wiener Neustadt, Canada, through her embassy, accorded the refugees a sincere welcome. The Canadian ambassador to Austria, J.S. MacDonald, told the assembled 1,300 Hungarians who were to leave for Canada on December 27 that Canada admired the heroic people of Hungary as they attempted to restore "liberty" in their country. In a Christmas-bedecked room the Canadian ambassador extended a warm welcome to the refugees in the following words:

> We extend to you who have been driven from your home-land under such harrowing circumstances, an opportunity to begin a new career... We offer you also the opportunity of taking part with us in the building up, far from strife-torn Europe, a new Canadian nation...[183]

When the refugees arrived in Canada they were given special attention and care. Immigration centres across Canada sheltered, fed and met the immediate needs of the refugees. Through the National Employment Service (NES) they were provided with an opportunity to find suitable employment. Unlike the Anders army veterans, and like the Czechoslovakian refugees, the Hungarian refugees were not obliged to work on the farm before they were accepted as landed immigrants. Besides the help given by National Employment Service (NES), organizations and individuals also gave them a helping hand by offering temporary lodgings.

As noted before, Pickersgill made arrangements with the United Kingdom, France and Netherlands to look after the refugees destined for Canada until the summer had arrived in Canada. United Kingdom looked after 5,000 refugees; France, 3,000 and Netherlands, 2,000.[184]

The same enterprising Pickersgill made arrangements with 33 universities to take in Hungarian students. Some universities assisted the students with the payment of tuition, the cost of books

---

[183]J.S. MacDonald to USSEA, December 26, 1956, Department of External Affairs file #5475-EA-4-40, DEA.

[184]"Hungarian Refugee Movement", May 1, 1959, ibid.

and accommodation and food. A number of students received full four-year scholarships.

Besides the regular students, two groups of students and professors from the University of Sopron[185] were accepted by two Canadian universities. The first group, consisting of 190 students and 115 professors and dependents, were taken in by the University of British Columbia. The second group, consisting of 76 students and 39 professors and dependants, were accepted by the University of Toronto.

The change of Canadian government in 1957 did not drastically alter the Canadian refugee policy. However, minor changes were made by the new Conservative government because of the growing unemployment. There was another factor involved. Other national groups, particularly the Italians, were seeking an entry into Canada. After several cabinet meetings on the subject of the Hungarian refugee movement, the government agreed to restrict transportation assistance except for those who filed an application for admission to Canada or for whom the sponsors filed before April 30, 1958. Free transportation was provided only if the refugee arrived prior to December 31, 1958.[186] But these detailed regulations were dropped, however, when the Canadian government, responding to the urgent appeal from the United Nations High Commission for Refugees, decided to take in 3,400 more Hungarian refugees.[187]

Altogether to the end of December 31, 1958, 37,566 Hungarian refugees arrived in Canada: 4,167 in 1956; 31,851 in 1957 and 1,548 in 1958.[188] For some reasons, slightly more than one half of the original number suggested by the United Nations High Commission for Refugees came to Canada in 1958. Out of nearly 38,000 refugees only 459 were repatriated to Hungary at the expense of the Canadian government.

Thus the saga of bringing hope to thousands of Hungarian refugees proved to be a glorious moment in Canadian history. The

---

[185]Memorandum to the Cabinet, June 30, 1958, *ibid*.

[186]"Hungarian Refugees", Cabinet conclusion, October 4, 1957, Privy Council Office, Management Branch, Ottawa, p. 7.

[187]"Hungarian Refugees", Cabinet Conclusion, July 14, 1958, *ibid*.

[188]"Hungarian Refugee Movement", May 1, 1959, Department of External Affairs, file "5475-EA-4-40, DEA.

treatment of these refugees attested to the generosity of the Canadian people. To a certain extent the humanitarian treatment of the Hungarians compensated for the insensitive attitude of the Canadian government to the veterans of General Anders army and Canada's lukewarm policy shown towards the victim of Nazi persecution.

Regular Immigration

Besides the great influx of refugees and displaced persons who entered Canada during the post-World War II period, there were also many regular immigrants. Until 1956, most East European countries discouraged emigration on the grounds that they needed all available manpower to re-construct their own country. Table IV contains not only the regular immigration figures but also the displaced persons and refugees. During the years, 1946-48, immigration from East European countries was negligible. The large Czechoslovakian immigration figure includes the refugees after the Czech *coup*, and so do the figures for Hungary in the 1956-62 period contain approximately 37,000 Hungarian refugees. After the Soviet-Yugoslav break, many of the Yugoslavs were permitted to emigrate to the West, including Canada. Hence the large immigration figures for the periods 1959-55 and 1956-62. The gradual liberalization in Eastern Europe permitted more of the nationals to join their relatives in the West. Poland is, perhaps, the best example of a country which began to put into effect the policy of family re-unification. This policy allowed many of the East Europeans to join their relatives

Regular Immigration*

Table IV

	1946-48	1949-55	1956-62
Bulgarians	74	775	232
Czechoslovakians	1,944	8,698	285
Hungarians	1,325	10,808	40,566
Poles	17,223	44,204	18,668

Table IV

Romanians	585	2,742	1,073
Ukrainians	12,177	22,170	2,225
Yugoslavians	3,025	13, 705	23,738

*This is based on data from Statistics Section, Department of Citizenship and Immigration, Ottawa.

Regular immigration to Canada from Eastern Europe was different from regular immigration from Western countries. Because of the communist regimes in the East European countries, there was always the possibility that some of the immigrants might be sent to Canada by their respective governments to carry on espionage. And even the immigrants who were not members of the communist parties, but who had spent five to ten years in a communist state where full scale indoctrination of the mind was a policy of the government might have tainted them somewhat ideologically. No immigrant from Eastern Europe received his or her visa to come to Canada until he or she received security screening.[189] Generally, security screening was waived when the proposed immigrants were wives of bone fide immigrant husbands. The same regulation held true for children under 18, widows with children under 18, children 16 years of age accompanied by adults, men 65 years old and over, women over 60, priests, clergymen and other recognized members of an organized religious body.

Most of the East European countries wanted Canadian immigration officers to be stationed in legations, in order to process the applicants faster, particularly applications of those the communist regime wanted to emigrate. The Canadian government, on the other hand, did not want to give the people the impression by stationing such an officer that everyone who applied would be accepted.

---

[189]"Security Screening," n.d. department of Citizenship and Immigration, RG. 76 vol. 800, file #5471, National Archives of Canada, Ottawa.

Chapter VI

Commercial Relations
with Eastern Europe

Canada relies very heavily on her external trade. She needs markets for her agricultural, industrial, mineral and forest products. Approximately 70 percent of her trade has been and still is with her southern neighbor, the United States. Being a member of the British Commonwealth where she received preferential tariff treatment, she did have a considerable amount of trade with such countries as the United Kingdom, Australia, New Zealand and South Africa. Her trade with Western Europe was competing with her British Commonwealth trade. However, her trade with Eastern Europe had never been significant until she began to sell wheat in the mid fifties to these countries of Europe.

One of the reasons for Canada's opening of legations in Czechoslovakia, Poland and Yugoslavia was to increase trade. Canada's representatives were given instruction to encourage commercial relations. That was not always easy, as many of the East European countries produced the same kind of products Canada wanted to sell. There was also the problem of currency. Most of the East European countries were in dire need of Western currency since currencies from Eastern European countries were not accepted in the West. In the post-World War II period countries of Eastern Europe carried on their export-import trade more with the Soviet Union than with Western countries.

The Export-Import trade between Canada and East European Countries indicating the size of the trade.* (1938)

Table I

	Canada's Exports	Canada's Imports
Bulgaria	$9,000	less than $500
Czechoslovakia	$3,164,000	$2,528,000
Hungary	$4,000	$161,000
Poland	$1,035,000	$261,000
Romania	$42,000	$44,000
Yugoslavia	$12,000	$64,000

*Dominion Bureau of Statistics, *Canada Year Book 1950*, Ottawa.

Post-War Years

The Second World War disrupted trade between Canada and the rest of the world including Eastern Europe. Canada severed relations with Nazi Germany and her satellites. Before the final victory in Europe, Canada began to pour in millions of dollars of relief for the rehabilitation of Europe. Most of this assistance was channelled through the United Nations Relief and Rehabilitation Administration (UNRRA). Table II indicates the extent of this assistance. Imports from the above three countries were negligible for the years 1945 and 1946, but in 1947 Czechoslovakia exported over three million dollars worth of goods to Canada.

Canada's Exports To:*

Table II

	1945	1946	1947
Czechoslovakia	$6,717,000	$9,871,000	$13,799,027

Table II

Poland	$9,249,195	$2,2501,000	$15,379,502
Yugoslavia	$11,710,521	$12,030,000	$6,728,829

*Dominion Bureau of Statistics, *Canada Year Book 1950*, Ottawa

Canada's Imports From:*

Table III

	1945	1946	1947
Czechoslovakia	Nil	$964,000	$3,644,843
Poland	Nil	$847,308	$2,732
Yugoslavia	Nil	$ 2,000	$22,548

*Dominion Bureau of Statistics, *Canada Year Book 1950*, Ottawa.

In general, Canadian aid consisted of food material, medical supplies, machinery and clothing. By 1947, assistance under the United Nations Relief and Rehabilitation Administration (UNRRA) was discontinued by the United States and United Kingdom because the Soviet Union did not want the UNRRA officials to distribute the food and supplies. Canada was forced to follow suit, although she did have $20 million to give in post-UNRRA relief. Countries earmarked for such an aid were Albania, Austria, Czechoslovakia, Greece, Italy, Poland, the Soviet Union and Yugoslavia. Of all the countries, Poland was singled out to receive the greatest share of Canada's post-UNRRA relief. Some of the cabinet members felt that the communist regime in Poland would probably give this aid to the supporters of the regime rather than to needy people. After much thought the Canadian government decided to give 5 million dollars to Poland, funneled through the UNICEF and the remainder distributed among such pro-western countries as Austria, Greece and Italy.[190]

---

[190]John W. Holmes, *The Shaping of Peace, 1953-57*, vol. I, Toronto, 1979, pp. 86-87

Restricted Commercial Relations

The Soviet Union through its Red Army, its secret police and the national communist parties had by 1948 consolidated its control over Eastern Europe. Even the semi-democratic state of Czechoslovakia fell into the hands of the communists in 1948. In other East European countries the communist-front social democratic parties were absorbed into the communist parties. Elections were held as a single Party list of candidates and were presented to the general public. In each East European country secretaries of the communist parties were selected with the assistance of Moscow. Party members were bound to strict discipline in implementing the decisions of the party elite. Through the party system, trade unions, collective farms and state enterprises were controlled.

The Soviet Union exploited her satellites economically. For instance, Poland was required to sell her coal at a price below that of the world market level. With the formation of the Council of Mutual Economic Aid, commonly called COMECON, in January, 1949, a concerted effort was made to coordinate economic and commercial policies of the Soviet bloc countries. Moscow continued to emphasize the concept of economic reliance on the Soviet bloc, rather than on national self-determination.

Western powers became increasingly alarmed by the Soviet domination of Eastern Europe. The Czech *coup* of February, 1948 and the threat on Norway's independence galvanized the opposition to Soviet imperialism and initiated the formation of the North Atlantic Treaty Organization (NATO). As a military alliance, NATO was concerned with the shipment of strategic supplies to the Soviet Union or to her satellites. Each member of NATO passed legislation to control the export of such material. In Canada the Export-Import Permits Act provided authority to ensure that "articles having strategic nature or value" would not be used detrimentally to the security of Canada.[191] Strategic material included "arms, ammunitions, implements of war and such commodities as steel, ferrous and non-ferrous metals, minerals, and

---

[191]*Revised Statutes of Canada*, 1970, vol. 3, Queen's Printer, Ottawa, p. 2910.

(sic) chemicals and manufactured products which have a significant usage in defence industries."[192]

There persisted a problem of a clear definition of strategic goods. Broadly speaking, most goods could be considered as strategic. Even wheat could be so classified, for it not only could feed common people but armies as well.

There were other problems hampering trade with Eastern Europe. Western firms and enterprises had to deal with government agencies rather than with individual enterprises. Many times such transactions were time and energy consuming. Generally speaking, foreign trade in Eastern Europe was conducted with ten to twenty foreign trade monopolies which determined the kind and the amount of goods to be bought or sold annually.[193] In these countries the importing organizations and the distributing organizations were separate. The users of the product or those who would eventually use the product[194] helped in planning the imports and in approving the exports. In Czechoslovakia, Hungary, Bulgaria, Romania and to some extent in Poland, trade was centralized in the hands of large trading enterprises; one for each product. In Yugoslavia, a number of trading companies operated and competed with one another.[195]

Canadian commercial counsellors from Vienna and Copenhagen made periodic visits to the East European countries, where they investigated the needs of these enterprises, discovered what these enterprises had for sale and then began negotiating terms of agreement. Advertising Canadian products, as was done in Western Europe, would have little effect since the buyers were government agencies and not private individuals or enterprises. However, international fairs proved rather successful in creating an appetite

[192]*Canada, Debates of the House of Commons*, February 15, 1954, p. 2077. Queen's Printer, Ottawa.

[193]Peter A. Freyseng, Assistant Commercial Secretary, Vienna, "Advertising Abroad," *Foreign Trade*, Department of Trade and Commerce, February 11, 1961, p. 6.

[194]The end users may include the management, engineer, technicians and foremen of factories and state farms; directors and experts of national and provincial research institutes; officials of the state investment banks who influence the allocation of funds for important investment goods and officials of production ministries, *ibid*. p. 7.

[195]R.K. Thomson, Commercial Counsellor in Vienna, "How to travel in Eastern Europe," *Foreign Trade*, March 25, 1961, Department of Trade and Commerce, pp. 17-20.

for certain kinds of goods. One of the earliest fairs in which Canada participated was the Poznan fair of 1957. At this fair Canada displayed the Eldorado "60" Cobalt Beam Therapy Unit along with small displays of kitchen and laundry equipment. In 1959 Canada participated in the Brno trade fair and in 1960 in the Zagreb International Fair.

Such fairs did not eliminate the necessity of personal contacts by Canadian commercial counsellors, who would travel to the East European countries from their bases in Vienna and Copenhagen. Commercial counsellors visits lasting from four to five days kept a pulse on the needs of state corporations.

Table IV:* Canada's Exports to (In $1,000)

Table IV

	1948-1950	1951-1955
Bulgaria	$ 617	$ 23
Czechoslovakia	$16,604	$ 2,339
Hungary	$ 981	$ 359
Poland	$ 9,181	$ 4,909
Romania	$ 900	$ 621
Yugoslavia	$ 3,802	$ 34,774

*Dominion Bureau of Statistics, *Canada Year Book 1950*, 1956, Ottawa.

Canada's trade relations with Eastern Europe reflected the over-all East-West relations. Whenever the East-West relations were tense, Canada's possibilities of increasing trade was meagre but whenever there was an atmosphere of relaxation between East and West, all aspects of Canada's relations with Eastern Europe, including commercial, improved.

Table V: * Canada's Imports from (in $1,000)

Table V

	1948-1950	1951-1955
Bulgaria	$ 5	$ 9
Czechoslovakia	$17,246	$15,492
Hungary	$ 215	$ 918
Poland	$ 562	$ 3,230
Romania	$ 41	$ 45
Yugoslavia	$ 171	$ 1,151

*Dominion Bureau of Statistics, *Canada Year Book 1950*, 1956 Ottawa.

Tables IV and V indicate certain trends in the bilateral trade. Although the Czech *coup* inaugurated a new phase of the Cold War, it did not affect Czechoslovakian trade with Canada for the years 1948, 1949 and 1950. The long range contracts negotiated prior to 1948, could explain this consistent amount of imports. There is a significant drop in the amount of Canadian exports to Czechoslovakia in the years 1951-1955, possible because of the *coup*.

Poland's trade with Canada from 1948 until the first large purchase of wheat in 1955 was rather small. The 1948 export of Canadian products amounting to over five and one-half millions of dollars was largely made up of the UNRRA assistance. This was also true with the Canadian exports to Yugoslavia.

In 1946 Poland asked Canada for a loan so that she could purchase capital goods necessary for her recovery. The then under-secretary of state for External Affairs held that such credits would be of strategic importance if it enabled Poland to become a viable and independent country. However, he doubted whether Poland's independence would increase by such a loan.[196] The department of

---

[196]Norman Robertson to W.C. Clark, deputy minister of Finance, March 11, 1946, RG. 20, vol. 953, file #7-826, NAC.

Trade and Commerce argued against the granting of such a loan for other reasons.[197] In the view of the department the three million dollar loan would be of little assistance to Poland. With a tight control of the press, this loan would not be advertised so that the people would not give Canada the credit she deserved. Secondly, the loan was to be used in the purchase of railway rolling stock of which Canada had a short supply. Finally, the United States had, after much thought, decided not to go through with her loan of 40 million dollars on the grounds that the prospect of a free independent Poland was increasingly growing dimmer and dimmer.

However, when it came to Czechoslovakia, where the prewar democratic institutions continued to flourish until 1948, Canada did not hesitate to give a credit of 19 million dollars.[198] A good portion of this loan was translated into purchases of Canadian products. There seemed to be a limit to Canada's generosity even to further democratic elements in Czechoslovakia, for she declined to grant her an additional thirty million dollars as requested.[199]

The year when the Czechoslovakian relations with the West received a blow by the Czech *coup*, the Yugoslavian relations with the West began to expand. The rift between Tito and Stalin made this expansion possible. The newly appointed Canadian minister to Belgrade, Émile Vaillancourt, met with the Yugoslav minister of Foreign Affairs and discussed the possibility of trade.[200] Yugoslav needed such capital goods as mining paper & agricultural machinery, and railway and road construction equipment. The Canadian minister assured the Yugoslav minister that Canada would be too glad to supply these goods. Unfortunately, Yugoslavia did not have hard currency to pay for them and Canada did not accept a network of barter and partial payment arrangements.

Two Years later, in May 1950, Yugoslav ministers to Ottawa and to Washington met with the Canadian members of the depart-

---

[197]Memorandum of the Department of Trade and Commerce, May 17, 1946, RG. 20, vol. 953, file #7-826. Norman Robertson argued that "Canada should not follow the United States, for after all, the United States would not make their course dependent on our cooperation, so I see no reasons why we should commit ourselves."

[198]Memorandum prepared by R.T. Young, Department of Trade and Commerce, January 14, 1947, RG. 20, vol. 1027, file #18-177.

[199]H.H. Wrong, acting under-secretary of state for External Affairs, to Frantisek Pavlasek, Czechoslovak minister to Canada, June 17, 1946, *ibid.*

[200]J.P. Manion, commercial secretary to G.R Heasman, May 5, 1948, *ibid.*

ments of Trade and Commerce, Finance and External Affairs to discuss how trade between the two countries could be increased.[201] The Yugoslav representatives anticipating the financial hurdle assured the Canadian officials that Yugoslavia received loans from the United States and from the International Bank enabling her to pay for her exports. At the same time they urged Canada to help bring about a better balance in the export-import trade by buying Yugoslav wood products, wines and handicrafts. Indeed, trade did increase but the balance was not rectified, for in 1955 Yugoslavia bought twenty-five times more from Canada than she exported to Canada. (See Tables IV and V).

During the period from 1948 to 1955 Canada's export-import trade with Bulgaria, Hungary and Romania was consistently lower than that with Czechoslovakia, Poland and Yugoslavia. During the years 1948 and 1949 Bulgarian exports to Canada were less that $500. Romania's exports were somewhat higher than those of Bulgaria and Hungary's were the highest of the three countries. Canada's main exports to these countries at this period of time were capital goods and medical supplies.

International Atmosphere
and Commercial Relations, 1956-1962

The death of Stalin caused a lessening of tensions between the East and the West. With the Soviet dictator gone, a breathing space was created in Eastern Europe as each communist country attempted to allow some freedom without upsetting the delicate balance existing between these countries and the Soviet Union. The famous speech of Nikita Khruschev to the Twentieth Party Congress of the Soviet Union in 1956 expressed openly the feelings of many Russians. Stalin was condemned for decimating the Communist Party of the Soviet Union, for executing many able army officers and murdering thousands and thousands of people. This public denunciation of the "iron" man made it easier for the satellite countries to express their dissatisfaction with the Stalinist regimes. Some of this dissatisfaction was expressed in a quiet man-

---

[201]Memorandum prepared by G.A. Newman, to all Commodity Staff of the Department Of Trade and Commerce, May 6, 1950, Department of Trade and Commerce, National Archives of Canada, Ottawa.

ner, whereas other was characterized by protests and revolts. Students and intellectuals, particularly in Poland and Hungary, led the demands for reforms in the fields of economy, government, education and living conditions. The strong hand rule in East Germany, Romania, Bulgaria and Czechoslovakia prevented similar outbursts of protest against the Stalinist regimes.

Whereas the riots in Pozan, Poland, brought about the rise of a more liberal regime under Wladyslaw Gomulka, the revolt in Hungary to initiate a repressive regime under the leadership of Janos Kadar. Despite his condemnation of Stalin, Khruschev did not hesitate to crush the Hungarian quest for freedom and national independence, to scuttle the summit conference of 1960, initiated the Berlin crisis of 1961 and the Cuban crisis of 1962. The ebullient Soviet leader renewed the Cold War atmosphere.

At home, Khruschev initiated some far-reaching changes as he attempted to make his regime more efficient. Greater autonomy was given to local levels of administration in order to increase production and to eliminate some of the bureaucratic inefficiency. The new regime reduced the power of the secret police and slightly extended freedoms of speech and of movement.

This attitude of liberalization spread to Eastern Europe. Under this umbrella trade between Eastern Europe and the West increased, family reunification was encouraged, as many Poles, Yugoslavs, Romanians, and Bulgarians visited the West. In most countries of Eastern Europe there was less censorship of the mail and of telephone messages.

New Canadian Commercial Agreements with Eastern Europe

By 1965, Canada had concluded trade agreements and had exchanged the most-favoured-nation (MFN) treatment with all the Eastern bloc countries except with Romania. Canada negotiated with Czechoslovakia a Convention of Commerce providing MFN treatment based on the Agreement of March 15, 1928.[202] In 1948 both of these countries acceded to the General Agreement on Tariffs and Trade (GATT). In 1928 Canada had also adhered to a

---

[202]*The Canadian Annual Review, 1927-1928*, Toronto, p. 288.

Treaty of May 12, 1928, negotiated between the United Kingdom and the Kingdom of Serbs-Croats-Slovenes. Canada adhered to this treaty by a Convention of Commerce negotiated on June 11, 1928.[203] This Convention continued to govern trade between the two countries in the post-World War II period. All goods bought or exchanged by Canada and Yugoslavia received MFN treatment.

Canada and Poland signed a commercial treaty on July 3, 1935, and the Canadian government ratified it two days later.[204] Canadian-Polish trade relations were also governed by a Convention of Commerce, made effective on August 15, 1936. This Convention provided a mutual MFN treatment. Poland participated in GATT under a special declaration of November 9, 1959. Bulgaria concluded a three year trade agreement with Canada on October 8, 1963, providing a MFN treatment. A similar three year agreement was negotiated with Hungary on June 11, 1964.[205]

One of the first East European countries to buy wheat from Canada was Yugoslavia. In 1954 she made a six million dollar purchase of wheat.[206] With the reconciliation between Tito and Khruschev, more and more of the needed wheat came from the Soviet Union. By 1959 the Yugoslav purchases from Canada became diversified as she not only bought wheat but also other Canadian products.

Czechoslovakia also purchased wheat from Canada in 1954. This first large grain purchase occurred after Canada agreed to terminate the anti-dumping tariffs on Czech imports into Canada.[207] The second purchase of wheat was negotiated in 1955. There were some difficulties in paying for the wheat. To buy the Canadian

[203]Legation of the Kingdom of Serbs-Croats-Slovenes in London, England to the Secretary of State for Foreign Affairs, Ottawa, file #T-11478, vol. 1, NAC.

[204]See Chapter V of Aloysius Balawyder, *The Maple Leaf and the White Eagle, Canadian-Polish Relations 1918,1978*, Boulder, 1980. The Polish Sejm ratified the Treaty on January 24, 1936, followed by the ratification by the Polish Senate on February 4, 1936.

[205]C.R.D. Kelley, "Canada's Trade Relations with Eastern Europe", *Foreign Trade*, CXXIV, August 7, 1965, pp. 20-21.

[206]C.M. Isbister, assistant deputy minister of Trade and Commerce to L. Couillard, head of Economic Division of department of External Affairs, January 22, 1957, department of External Affairs (hereafter referred to as DEA) file #9035-40, DEA.

[207]Memorandum for the minister to department of External Affairs, July 27, 1959, DEA file #7670-40, DEA.

wheat the Czechoslovakian ministry of Foreign Trade received necessary funds from the Czechoslovak state bank. The ministry of Foreign Trade could not receive further loans until the previous loans were paid.[208]

Table VI:* Canada's Exports to: (in $1,000)

Table VI

	1956-1958	1959-1962
Bulgaria	$ 288	$ 1,356
Czechoslovakia	$ 27,283	$ 47,880
Hungary	$ 2,580	$ 2,960
Poland	$ 35,095	$106,506
Romania	$ 1,723	$ 4,034
Yugoslavia	$ 593	$ 8,960

*Dominion Bureau of Statistics, *Canada Year Book* 1963-64, Ottawa.

Table VII:* Canada's Imports from (in $1,000):

Table VII

	1956-1958	1959-1962
Bulgaria	$ 8	$ 70
Czechoslovakia	$ 15,570	$ 30,532
Hungary	$ 1,058	$ 1,358
Poland	$ 4,340	$ 11,498
Romania	$ 6	$ 441
Yugoslavia	$ 2,277	$ 4,821

**Dominion Bureau of Statistics, *Canada Year Book 1963-64*, Ottawa.

---

[208]Conversation with J. Votruba, November 12, 1958, DEA file #7670-40, DEA.

In the late 1950s, Czechoslovakia tried desperately to obtain credits from Canada. One of the Czechoslovakian commercial counsellors, J. Votruba, based in Ottawa, did his utmost to persuade Canadian authorities to grant his country 10 million dollars over a period of three to five years with which to buy barley, raw materials and consumer goods. He claimed that Czechoslovakia would match the Canadian government loan by a Czech government loan to the Canadian provinces. Both of these schemes, he said, would be a mutual commitment to purchase goods for a total value equivalent to the loans. He encouraged the Canadian government to make loans to small businesses in order to promote export sales.[209]

The Canadian government made it clear to the Czech counsellor that Canada was not in a position to make loans. However, the deputy minister of the department of Trade and Commerce assured the counsellor that Canada was vitally interested in selling goods to Czechoslovakia. He suggested that Canada warmly welcomed a Czech trade mission and a Czech trade officer in Toronto as a means of increasing Czecho-Canadian trade. As most of East European trade missions, a Czechoslovakian trade office in Toronto raised security considerations.[210] After a study the RCMP did not consider such a trade office a serious security risk.

The Czechoslovakian government placed pressure on Canada to reciprocate such a move by its appointment of a commercial representative in Prague. Czechoslovakia had a market for such Canadian products as nickel, asbestos, antibiotics, barley and wheat. The Canadian commercial counsellor, R.K. Thomson, operating from Vienna, pointed out that while Czechoslovakia had probably the largest potential market for Canadian goods among the six countries within his territory (most of the East European countries and Austria), the extent to which this potential could develop would depend on Czechoslovakian policy to expand her exports to Canada rather than on the work of any commercial counsellor.[211] After some discussion between the Canadian legation in Prague, the department of External Affairs and the department

---

[209]F.P. Weiser to M. Schwarzman, Director, International Trade Relations Branch, September 29, 1958, DEA, file #7670-40E, *ibid.*

[210]John H. English, deputy minister of Trade and Commerce, to Norman Robertson, USSEA, June 10, 1959, *ibid.*

of Trade and Commerce, it was decided that at that time, having a Canadian commercial representative permanently in Prague was not justified.[212]

Wheat Deals with Poland

Although Czechoslovakia offered markets for diversified Canadian products, Poland became the most important market for Canadian wheat and barley. The Canadian-Polish trade negotiations seemed to proceed much smoother than the Canadian-Czechoslovak negotiations. There appeared to be certain reasons for this. First of all, all discussion was carried out in English as both the chairman and the commercial counsellor of the Polish delegation conversed in perfect English thus eliminating the possibility of misinterpretation.[213] Unlike the Czech counterparts, the Polish officials were exceedingly well versed in the knowledge of Canadian regulations dealing with custom duties, financing and policies of private businessmen.[214]

The 1955 purchase of Canadian wheat was a straight forward commercial transaction. Canada sold 250,000 tons of wheat to Poland on terms of 15% cash at the time of purchase with the balance payable within twelve months. The Canadian government, through the Export Credit Insurance corporation, insured the exporter.[215] A year later Poland purchased 200,000 tons of Canadian wheat under terms similar to that of 1955.[216]

The two large purchases of grain created an imbalance in trade with Poland. Canada bought very little from Poland,

[211]R.K. Thomson to the assistant deputy minister of the external trade promotion, July 21, 1960, *ibid*.

[212]USSEA to the deputy minister of National Revenue, October 31, 1960, *ibid*.

[213]A.E. Ritchie to the Canadian legation in Warsaw, August 5, 1955, DEA file #9533-40, DEA. The chairman was Ludwik Dobrzanski and the commercial attaché was Artur Zyto.

[214]*Ibid*.

[215]Minister for the minister of External Affairs, July 6, 1958, DEA file #9533-40, DEA.

[216]"Export Credits to Poland for Purchase of Wheat," Cabinet Conclusion, January 25, 1956, Privy Council Office, Management Branch, Ottawa.

although the latter urged Canada to buy her hams, ceramic products, leather, textile goods, and fishing boats.[217]

Canada understood this dilemma. On another level her officials at home and abroad attempted to discreetly encourage Poland's separate road to socialism as envisioned by Gomulka. Attempts were made to lessen her dependency on the Soviet Union. If there was a choice for Canada to make as to what East European country she should and could assist through the extension of credits, the under-secretary of state for External Affairs felt it ought to be Poland. For instance, he argued that Poland deserved greater support than Romania, for the latter showed little signs of lessening its ties with the Kremlin.[218] At the same time he saw no objection of any sale of wheat to Romania as such but, given the choice of extending credits and given the fact that a substantial portion of $100,000,000 guaranteed under Section 21 of the Export Credit Insurance Act was already committed, he felt that Poland should be given the preference.[219]

Canada showed her sympathy for Poland's plight in another way. She deferred the payment of 12.5 million debt for one year.[220] A similar deferment of debt settlement was accorded to Yugoslavia in 1956 as she too showed signs of drawing away from the Soviet Union.

Satisfied with Poland's prompt payment of debts, Canada entered into two other wheat agreements, one in 1956-57 and the other in 1957-58. The arrangements for the payment of these two large purchases were somewhat modified. The initial payment was to be 10% followed by a payment of 30% after two and one-half years and the final payment of 30% to be made at the end of three years.[221] Significantly, Canada required Poland to pay 10% of the

---

[217]J.P. Erichsen-Brown to USSEA, October 23, 1956, DEA file #9533-40. DEA. "Export Credits to Poland for Purchase of Wheat," Cabinet Conclusion, January 25, 1956, Privy Council Office, Management Branch, Ottawa.

[218]Jules Leger, USSEA, to K.W. Taylor, deputy minister of Finance, November 14, 1956, ibid.

[219]Memorandum for the minister of department of External Affairs, January 10, 1957, ibid.

[220]"Wheat sales to Poland; export credit guarantees", January 17, 1957, Privy Council Office, Management Branch, Ottawa. Part of the payment was postponed for six months and the remainder for one year.

cost in the initial payment, whereas the Czechs were required to pay 25% of the payment.

One of the difficulties encountered by Poland in buying Canadian wheat was the individual negotiations that took place with each grain exporter. Poland suggested that this could be remedied by a government-to-government transaction.[222] Canada agreed to this, but she declined to lower the down payment to 5 percent. However, the Canadian government authorized the Export Credit Insurance to provide Poland with the necessary credits to purchase more grain.[223] Accordingly, Poland bought 150,000 tons of barley and 100,000 tons of wheat valued at $17,000,000 during the crop year, 1959/60.[224] Another purchase under similar terms was made in 1961 when 300,000 tons of Canadian wheat were sold to Poland.[225]

Poland continued to buy Canadian wheat in subsequent years. The post-World War II population boom, coupled with crop failures and inefficient agricultural methods made such large purchases necessary. The detention of the Polish Art Treasures hampered somewhat the wheat transaction, but not to a large extent. Canada attempted in every way to encourage Poland's road to its own brand of socialism by loans and by deferment of payment of debts.[226]

---

[221]"Wheat: export to Poland", Cabinet Conclusion, March 14, 1957, Privy Council Office, Management Branch, Ottawa.

[222]Under section 21 of the Exports Credits Insurance Act, the Canadian government insured the banks against the non-payment of the buyers. This allowed the Canadian exporters to arrange the necessary financing through commercial banks and other institutions. From the fall of 1952 to November 2, 1957, approximately $136 millions worth of wheat have been exported under such an arrangement.

[223]Memorandum to Cabinet re "Sale of wheat and barley to Poland under section 21 of the Export Credits Insurance Act," November 2, 1959, Privy Council Office, Management Branch, Ottawa.

[224]Ibid., pp. 2-4.

[225]Memorandum to Cabinet re "Sale of wheat under section 21 of the Export Credit Insurance Act," September 5, 1961. DEA file #9533-40, DEA.

[226]Ibid.

Canadian-Hungarian Commercial Relations

Hungary too asked Canada for a most-favoured-nation treatment similar to that accorded the Soviet Union on February 29, 1956. Canada agreed to grant this to Hungary on October 3, 1956. According to the agreement, Hungary was to buy about $150,000 worth of wheat each year for over a period of three years. At least 50,000 tons were to be purchased each year. However, equal quantities of barley or wheat flour could be substituted for wheat.[227] An agreement was reached whereby Hungary would open a trading agency in Montreal and Canada would eventually open one in Budapest.[228]

The Hungarian Revolution stalled Canada's signing of the agreement. However, some cabinet members favoured such a signing on the grounds that the sale of wheat would help the victims of the Revolution; others argued that a sale of wheat backed by Canadian credits could be interpreted as a move favouring the policies of the new communist regime.[229]

The Hungarian government approached the Canada Wheat Board in May 1957 to buy wheat without signed agreement. The Canada Wheat Board responded that no sale of wheat could be made without the signing of a trade agreement, and that such endorsement would not be made until and unless the political climate in Hungary was substantially altered.[230] Moreover, Canada was displeased with the unfriendly references made to her treatment of Hungarian refugees.[231] In accordance with the NATO policies, Canada refrained from any move which could be interpreted as a support for the new Hungarian regime.[232]

---

[227]"Trade with Hungary". Cabinet Conclusion, October 3, 1956, Privy Council Office, Management Branch, Ottawa.

[228]Memorandum, for the Cabinet, "Proposed Trade Agreement with Hungary", October 24, 1956, *ibid.*

[229]"Trade Agreement with Hungary", Cabinet Conclusion, January 7, 1957, *ibid.*

[230]"Trade Agreement with Hungary", Memorandum for the Minister, May 7, 1957, DEA files #9376-A-40, DEA.

[231]Hungarian enquiry concerning the possibility of signing the Trade Agreement. December 23, 1957, *ibid.*

[232]Under-secretary of state for External Affairs to the acting deputy minister of Trade and Commerce, *ibid.*

However, by 1961, the NATO powers began to alter their policy towards Hungary. France, United States and the United Kingdom were ready to enter into a trade agreement with Hungary. This opened the door for Canada. In March 1961 a three-man Hungarian delegation met in Ottawa with Canadian counterparts. The Hungarian delegation expressed a desire to buy 100,000 tons of wheat in return for an exchange of the most-favoured-nation tariff treatment.[233] Canada, on the other hand, was willing to sell the wheat on a cash basis only. The question of the most-favoured-nation treatment should, so argued the Canadian government, be decided between the Canada Wheat Board and the Hungarian officials.[234] When the Hungarian delegation refused to accept such a proposal, the wheat deal was shelved again.

In December 1961, the Hungarian officials approached the Canada wheat Board representatives in London and later Canada's High Commissioner to the United Kingdom about the possibility of a wheat purchase on a credit basis and a most-favoured-nation treatment (MFN) for Hungarian goods entering Canada. Canadian officials reiterated the Canadian policy that all purchases were to be on a cash basis and that Canada was not ready to accord Hungary a MFN treatment at that time.[235] Hungary repeated the same requests in February 1962 and again in September of the same year.

In November 1962, the Canadian government revised its policy towards Hungary. Ottawa felt that the new regime was now stabilized and that it desisted from criticizing the Canadian policy of acceptance of Hungarian refugees. In this general atmosphere, Canada was willing to grant Hungary credit to buy 250,000 tons of Canadian wheat for which 10 percent was to be paid in cash and the remainder to be paid over a three year period.[236] Hungary was pleased with the Canadian credits but was disappointed with the exclusion of the MFN term. Hungary was so anxious to

---

[233]Proposed visit to Canada of Hungarian trade officials, April 11, 1961, *ibid.*

[234]"Trade with Hungary," Cabinet Conclusion, Privy Council, Management Branch, May 4, 1961, Management Branch, Ottawa.

[235]Memorandum regarding "Commercial Relations with Hungary," November 9, 1962, DEA file #9376-A-40.

[236]Memorandum to the Cabinet, November 6, 1962 *ibid.*

receive the MFN terms that she agreed to purchase six to seven million dollars worth of Canadian goods if Canada gave her the MFN treatment.[237]

It was not till 1964 that the package deal was concluded. Hungary purchased 250,000 tons of wheat valued at 19 million dollars, was accorded MFN terms and was permitted to establish a trade office in Montreal. Canada and Hungary agreed to establish diplomatic relations and to discuss consular and claims matters.[238]

Bulgarian and Romanian Commercial Relations

Compared with the volume and value of trade Canada had with Czechoslovakia, Poland or Yugoslavia, the trade with Bulgaria and Romania was very small. See Tables VI and VII. Canada's exports to Bulgaria included farm machinery, chemicals, newsprint, aluminum, tinplate, steel products, seeds and cattle.[239] Canada's exports to Romania included wool rags, nickel, aluminum, ingot, plastics, synthetic rubber, hybrid seed corn, purebred cattle, swine and breeding poultry.[240]

---

[237]Commercial relations with Hungary, November 7, 1962, *ibid*.

[238]C.F. Wilson, "Canada's Trade Relations with Eastern Europe," *Foreign Trade*, September 3, 1966. Department of Trade and Commerce, Ottawa, vol. CXXVI, pp. 2-4.

[239]R.K. Thomson, "Trading with Eastern Europe", *Foreign Trade*, July 14, 1962, Department of Trade and Commerce, pp. 32, 35.

[240]*Ibid*.

Chapter VII

Religious Persecution
in Eastern Europe

Religious persecution issue touched every East European satellite. Apart from the Hungarian Revolution, 1956, Canada had no significant relations with the Balkan countries during the years 1945-1962. The religious persecution brought Romania and Hungary into the Canadian sphere of interest because of the Peace Treaties that she signed in 1947 in which each of the signatories agreed to respect the human rights and fundamental freedoms of the people of their countries. Canada did not have such a treaty with Bulgaria.

Canada pursued with determination both bilaterally and through the offices of the United Nations a search concerning the scope of the religious persecution in these two Balkan countries and a means of persuading these countries to abide with the terms of the Treaties. The respect for human rights including the right to worship without fear was a principle dearly cherished by the Canadian public, most of whom were Christians.

When Canada took a vigorous stance against the religious persecution in Romania and Hungary, she equally decried similar persecution in Poland, Czechoslovakia (after 1948) and Yugoslavia. In all the East European satellites, communist regimes carried out a systematic persecution of believers. In line with the policies of the Soviet government, the satellite regimes considered all religions "opiate" of the people used to lessen respect and obedience to the state.

The methods employed to control religion varied from one country to country, from one denomination to another and from one time to another. The death of Stalin in 1953 and the rise of Nikita Khrushchev did not lessen the campaign against religions. Neither did Yugoslavia's rift with the Soviet Union measurably mitigate the concerted persecution of Catholics, Protestants, Orthodox Christians, and Muslims.

The nature of religious persecution were quite similar in each of the communist countries. The states insisted on nationalizing church property, restricting the teaching of religion in schools or public buildings, requiring seminarians to undergo a two year military training thus disrupting their formation; mandating that all religious rites associated with baptism and marriage would be preceded by civil functions; permitting abortion and divorce; demanding that all religious orders and priests become, more or less, servants of the state. Hundreds of priests, ministers, and nuns were arrested and jailed for alleged acts of treason.

Of all Christian churches, the Roman Catholic Church was usually targeted by constant harassment and persecution. The communists singled out the Catholics as rebels and disobedient to the wishes of the state. They argued that the Catholics who owed allegiance to the Pope in Rome could not be obedient servants of the State. In addition, the Catholic church adopted an uncompromising stance on matters of faith and morals, particularly in dealing with divorce, abortion and the right and duty of the parents to provide religious instruction of the children.

In all the East European satellites the communist regimes attempted to break this solidarity of the faithful believers by introducing pseudo organizations consisting of renegade priests or ministers who pretended to speak on behalf of their church. In such countries as Bulgaria, Romania and (Serbia) Yugoslavia, the communist regimes took advantage of the separate Orthodox national church organizations to persuade some of the Orthodox clergy and bishops to conform with the wishes of the regimes. In predominantly Catholic countries like Poland, Czechoslovakia and Hungary the communist regimes attempted to deprive the faithful of leaders by imprisoning the primates; Cardinal Wyszynski of

Poland, Cardinal Stepinac of Yugoslavia, Cardinal Mindszenty of Hungary and Archbishop Beran of Prague.[241] From time to time some of the members of parliament reminded the House of Commons of the continuous persecution of believers in the Soviet Union and in East European satellites. However, it was the trial and the arrest of Cardinal Mindszenty that sparked statements from the secretary of state for External Affairs and from the prime minister. Cardinal Mindszenty, a popular and a heroic figure, was subjected to a sham three day trial where there were no witnesses presented and where the defence did not challenge the prosecutor's unsubstantiated allegations of treason, espionage and illegal use of foreign currency.[242]

On January 26, 1949, Hume Wrong, the Canadian minister to Washington,[243] protested orally to the Hungarian minister in Washington, the unjust trial of Cardinal Mindszenty and the persecution of leaders of other Christian denominations. On February 2, 1949, the secretary of state for External Affairs, L.B. Pearson,[244] stated in the House of Commons that the Canadian government strongly condemned and deplored the religious persecution by the government of Hungary. Quoting a section of the note presented to the Hungarian minister in Washington by the Canadian minister, he pointed out that the Canadian government also deplores and finds it unacceptable to have the Senior Bishop of the Lutheran Church in Hungary arrested on charges similar to those levied at Mindszenty and sentenced to two years in prison. He also pointed out that the Senior Bishop of the Calvinist church was forced by the communist government to leave the country.

Almost three weeks later, Prime Minister, Louis St. Laurent,[245] elaborated on Pearson's statement by informing the House

---

[241]Memorandum on "The Church in Czechoslovakia," n.d., R.G. 25, acc. 83/84/ 268, Box 313, National Archives of Canada. and "On Communist Atrocities," June 14, 1954, Ethnic Archives, Ottawa.

[242]Statement made by prime minister Louis St. Laurent to the House of Commons, February 22, 1949, *Debates of the House of Commons,* February 22, 1949.

[243]Memorandum on "Religious Persecution in Eastern Europe," March 10, Department for External Affairs (hereafter DEA) files, NAC.

[244]Statement made by L.B. Pearson in the House of Commons, February 2, 1949, *Canada, Debates of the House of Commons,* February , 1949, King's Printer, Ottawa.

[245]Statement of prime minister, Louis St. Laurent, to the House of Commons, *Canada, Debates of the House of Commons,* February 22, 1949, *ibid.*

that the Canadian government was not going to sit idle but would seek "like minded governments, signatory to the Treaty on the character and desirability of further action that may be taken jointly or independently" against the governments of Romania and Hungary. The prime minister pointed out that there were several measures that could be taken. However, the effectiveness of these measures would, in the large part, depend on the Soviet Union, whose approval as a signatory of the Peace Treaties would be necessary.

One of the main measures to resolve the issue of religious persecution was to establish a commission of three to act "in regards to any dispute arising" from the execution or the interpretation of the Treaties. The majority decision of this commission was binding on the parties concerned.

There was another possibility; the dispute could be referred to the United Nations whose charter and the declaration of human rights cover the areas of repression and persecution. To ascertain the nature and the scope of the persecution, the prime minister, revealed that the Canadian chargé d'affaires in Prague, R.M. Macdonnell, would travel to Romania and Hungary. Macdonell's trip did not include Bulgaria, because Canada did not sign a Treaty with this state. The prime minister did point out that in Bulgaria fifteen Protestant leaders were indicted on the charge of espionage. In Czechoslovakia two members of the Greek Catholic Church were tried for an alleged espionage and in Poland twenty six priests were detained and eight arrested for having read in their churches a pastoral letter from a bishop who condemned the anti-religious actions of the government. Prime Minister St. Laurent ended his statement by promising that his government would "use whatever means [were] available to support every effort to assert the principles of religious and political liberty and to restore their practice."[246]

The Canadian government pressed on with haste in the execution of the programme suggested by the prime minister. On April 2, 1949, Canada formally associated with the notes of protest from the United Kingdom and the United States and informally with notes submitted to Bulgaria.[247] On October 22, 1949,

---

[246]*Ibid.*

Canada co-sponsored a resolution which was adopted by the General Assembly of the United Nations requesting the International Court of Justice to provide advisory opinion on four questions related with the establishment of a commission suggested by the Treaties with the Balkan countries.

The International Court of Justice delivered its advisory opinion in two parts; one on March 30 and the other on July 18, 1950.[248] To the first and second questions on whether the exchanges between the Balkan states and the signatories of the Treaties constituted an existence of dispute and whether the three Balkan states were obliged to appoint representatives to the commission, the answer was in the affirmative. The third question was whether the Secretary General of the United Nations could appoint a third member to the commission if the Balkan states refused to do so, the answer was in the negative. If the answer to the third question was negative, the answer to the fourth question remained also negative.[249]

The Balkan states had thirty days to respond to the advisory opinion of the International Court. The Canadian government referring to the judgement to the first two questions urged through the good offices of the British ministers in Budapest and Bucharest the Hungarian and the Romania governments to appoint members to the commission. The text to the Hungary government read as follows;[250]

> 1. His Majesty's Legation present their compliments to the Ministry of Foreign Affairs of Hungary and have the honour, on behalf of the Government of Canada to direct the Ministry's attention to the Advisory Opinion on the interpretation of the Peace Treaties with Bulgaria, Hungary and Romania, which was given by the International Court of Justice on March 30, 1950.

---

[247]Memorandum on "Religious Persecution in Eastern Europe," March 10, 1950, *op. cit.*

[248]Final Report of the *Ad hoc* Political Committee entitled: "Observance in Bulgaria, Hungary and Romania of Human Rights and Fundamental Freedoms," October 5, 1950, DEA files, NAC.

[249]*Ibid.*

[250]Press Release from the Department of External Affairs, May 2, 1950, Legal Division, File #7-DF-l (a), DEA.

2. In the light of the opinion, it is assumed that the Hungarian Government will now nominate its representative to the Peace Treaty Commission and will inform the Secretary General of the United Nations of the nomination in accordance with the United Nations General Assembly Resolution of October 22, 1949. It is further assumed that the Hungarian Government will also be willing to enter into consultation with the Canadian Government with a view to the appointment of a third member in accordance with Article 40 of the Treaty of Peace.

3. As His Majesty's Legation informed the Ministry of Foreign Affairs in their note of January 5, 1950, on behalf of the Government of Canada, the Canadian Government has appointed Rt. Hon. Justice J.L. Ilsley, P.C., as its representative on the proposed commission.

The Hungarian government acknowledged the receipt of the note but argued that the existing dispute was not within the jurisdiction of the International Court of Justice nor of the United Nations to make any such judgements.[251] The government of Romania did not submit a reply. The Soviet government agreed with the Hungarian reply claiming that Article 2(7) of the Charter on Human Rights precluded the International Court from delivery of any advisory opinion and furthermore the Charter did not contain any provisions which authorized the United Nations to discuss issues arising from World War II.[252]

Keeping in mind the responses of the Hungarian and the Soviet governments, the Canadian representative at the *ad hoc* United Nations Political Committee, Hughes Lapointe, on October 5, 1950, articulated Canada's position. He stated that Canada accepted the opinion of the International Court of Justice even though she had some reservations with regards to the advisory opinion of the Court; she was concerned that the judgement of the Court might permit defaulting parties to violate peace treaties. He emphasized that Canada was "deeply disturbed" ...at the evidence of police oppression, subversions of justice and terrorism which had come to [the department of External Affairs office] from these (Balkan) countries. Such acts of breach of the Treaties

---

[251]"Final Report of the *Ad hoc* Political Committee," *op.cit.*
[252]Ibid.

of peace, he contended "are contrary to the language and the spirit of the United Nations Charter and make a retrograde step from a civilized conduct."[253]

Since the Balkan states refused to nominate members to the commission and even refuted that there was any breach of the terms of the Peace Treaties, the Western members of the United Nations decided to vigorously condemn the violation of human rights in these states and to closely monitor further violations. The Australian representative at the United Nations moved a motion which contained these two provisions. The Australian motion was accepted by the *ad hoc* Political Committee of the United Nations by a vote of 39 in favour, 5 against and 12 abstentions.[254]

The Australian resolution did not help free Mindszenty from prison nor did lessen the violation of human rights in the Balkans. During the Hungarian revolution, 1956, Mindszenty was released from prison and took refuge in the American embassy to prevent the new communist regime from interning him again.

Persecution of churches continued in Eastern Europe under Nikita Khrushchev and his satellite servants. Canadian delegates at the United Nations kept reminding the member states of the communist denial of human rights including the right to worship as one pleased. On November 23, 1953, Alcid Cote, the Canadian representative at the United Nations, stated before the committee of the General Assembly that it was difficult to take the Soviet's and the satellite's contention that they wanted peace when they continued to permit persecutions of all kinds including religious ones.[255]

---

[253]Final Report of the *Ad hoc* Political Committee, *op.cit.*
[254]Final Report of the *Ad hoc* Political Committee, *op.cit.*
[255]"Religious Persecution in Communist Countries," December 27, 1954, *op.cit.*

Chapter VIII

CBC-IS — Psychological Instrument of Canadian Foreign Policy

Canada not only carried on trade with Eastern Europe on a restricted basis and permitted selective immigrants to enter her boundaries, but through the CBC-IS she took steps to encourage a Canadian quality of life in East European countries. Cut off from the Western world the people of Eastern Europe were not aware of the social, economic and political institutions found in the West. Canada along with the other Western countries hoped to bring to the attention of the people behind the Iron Curtain that there were alternatives to communist-controlled regimes. They also hoped to lessen the ties with the Kremlin by encouraging national determination.

Such a task was not easy. In every East European country the mass media was under the control of the state. In some of the countries there was a limited access to the Western journals and newspapers, whereas in others there was none. Communist controlled radios and later televisions did not permit the Western point of view. The only way such media could operate in these countries was from the outside in the form of foreign broadcasts. Early in the post-World War II years the British Broadcasting Corporation (BBC), the Voice of America (VOA) and the American supported Radio Free Europe (ARFE) beamed regular programmes to the people of Eastern Europe. The Canadian Broadcasting Corporation-International Service (CBC-

IS), adopted policies based on the British and the American broadcasting models.

Purposes of Propaganda

From time immemorial nations used diplomacy, economy and military force as means of statecraft. At times one was more important than the other and on occasions all three were employed. If negotiations failed to achieve a designed end, a threat of economic blockade sometimes brought the unwilling partner to the negotiating table. If that failed, military force was exercised. The fourth instrument of statecraft, propaganda, was utilized with varying degrees of success. During the Persian Wars, the Punic Wars, the Seven Years Wars, the Napoleonic Wars and the Franco-Prussian War, propaganda was used to demoralize the enemy by providing an exaggerated image of the strength of the defending state. This instrument became more refined during the Second World War and was used in the Post World War II period.

Perhaps the best example of the use of propaganda as means of statecraft was found in Nazi Germany. Dr. J. Goebbels, the minister of propaganda, used the radio and to some degree, pamphlets, to undermine the resistance of the people Hitler planned to dominate. The famous Lord Ha Ha attempted to frighten the allies by projecting an image of invincibility of Nazi Germany. The allies retaliated by presenting their point of view. The role of the BBC and the VOA was to correct the half-truths spread by the enemy and to sustain the morale of the allies.

The Canadian Psychological Warfare Committee was formed in June 1943.[256] It was approved by the Canadian cabinet in October of the same year. This Committee, composed of representatives of the department of External Affairs, the Wartime Information Board, the three armed services and the representative of the Canadian Broadcasting corporation prepared radio scripts and pamphlet material directed towards the enemy and enemy-occupied territories. Secondly, it helped to re-educate the German prisoners of war in Canada. In 1943, Canada was not equipped to

---

[256]G. de T. Glazebrook to Major Beswich, secretary of the Joint-Intelligence Committee, April 28, 1952, department of External Affairs (hereafter referred to as DEA) file #50182-40, DEA.

carry out the first part of the mandate, and therefore she relied on the services of the Office of War Information (an American agency) and on the BBC. But two years later the CBC-IS transmitted messages through a powerful station established in Sackville, New Brunswick. Its first broadcast was to the German prisoners of war.

The Canadian Psychological Warfare Committee continued to function in the post-war years. However, its function differed from its wartime programme. The Committee hoped to project to the post World War II world — a world aspiring for co-operation and peace, and an image of Canadian democratic ideals.

But the hoped-for peace did not materialize. The wartime partnership of the Western allies and the Soviet Union disintegrated over the issues of the Soviet domination of Eastern Europe and of the disposition of Germany. The glimpse of democracy in Poland was snuffed off by threats, bribery and trickery. One Eastern European country after another fell into the arms of the communists with the assistance of the Red Army and the Soviet secret police. The Czech *coup* of 1948 convinced the Western powers that the post war years created new problems. In 1949 the North Atlantic Treaty Organization was formed to counter the Soviet aggressive policy. The NATO members believed that the Soviet imperialism needed to be countered not only by a show of military strength and economic measures but also by propaganda.

Information Services

Following the Czech *coup*, the under-secretary of state for External Affairs, L.B. Pearson, called a meeting of the senior officials of his department. Davidson Dunton of the CBC was also invited.[257] Two items were agreed upon at this meeting, one that some practical means of transmission was needed to send information behind the iron curtain and two that the co-ordination of overseas broadcasting with the Canadian foreign policy was essential. The Czech service was altered by Ottawa to include historical material and political commentaries. Pearson elaborated on the

---

[257]Bernard J. Hibbitts, "The CBC International Service as a Psychological Instrument of Canadian Foreign Policy in the Cold War, 1948-63," M.A. thesis, Carleton University, Ottawa, 1981.

general policy of the CBC-IS when he appeared at the Standing Committee on External Affairs. He said that one of the aims of the CBC-IS was "to develop a policy to preserve peace, check the inroads of Soviet imperialism and to strengthen the morale, faith and the determination of many friends of freedom and democracy who live behind the iron curtain but whose voices are silenced."[258]

The CBC-IS expanded its services extensively, for by 1951 it broadcast overseas in fourteen languages: Czech, Slovak, Russian, Dutch, Danish, Finnish, Norwegian, Swedish, English, French, German, Italian, Portuguese and Spanish. The main broadcasts were directed towards Czechoslovakia, the United Kingdom, Russia, France, Germany, Austria and Italy. The contents of these broadcasts were as follows: 30.3% news items; 33.8% political and semi-political commentaries; 25.5% non-political and 10.3% music.[259] Some of these programmes were used by local French and German radio stations and to a limited extent, by the BBC.

The ad hoc committee was willing to follow the reasonable guidelines of NATO but refused to adhere to its uniform ideological warfare policy. In the opinion of Norman Robertson, the chairman of the committee, such a policy smacked of the communist Cominform organization — an organization distasteful to most people in Western and Eastern Europe.[260] The *ad hoc* committee agreed on the need to make the CBC-IS more effective. It was felt that its representatives ought to meet on more frequent bases with the representatives of the VOA and of the BBC. At these meetings, ideas were to be exchanged and the effectiveness of the broadcasts were to be discussed.

Closer to home, Ira Dilworth, the general supervisor of the International Service, was convinced that the CBC-IS's effectiveness lay in its close relationship with the department of External Affairs.[261] Thereupon the department of External Affairs agreed to

---

[258]L.B. Pearson, secretary of state for External Affairs, to the Standing Committee on External Affairs, Minutes of Proceedings, May 30, 1951, Queen's Printer, Ottawa.

[259]Minutes of a meeting of an *Ad hoc* Committee on Government Information Services, March 17, 1951, DEA file #50182-490, DEA, Ottawa.

[260]Minutes of a Meeting of an *Ad hoc* Committee on Government Services, March 1, 1951, *ibid*.

[261]L.A.D. Stephens, "Study of Canadian Government Information Culture and Academic Divisions and their Policies," department of External Affairs, Historical Division, 1977.

second Jack A. McCordick to CBC-IS, as a coordinator of the Canadian foreign policy directives for IS.

Another step was taken to place the International Service under fuller control of the department of External Affairs by the appointment in January 1952 of Jean Desy, former Canadian ambassador to Brazil, as the director general of the International Service. Charles Delafield, of the CBC, was made the assistant director general.[262]

Desy threw himself into the task of reforming the CBC-IS with righteous zeal. By the end of his eighteen month mandate there were many changes. Some members of the organization, who were "marking time," were released from the service, and others who could not tolerate Desy's autocratic regime resigned on their own.[263] His thorough assessment of the International Service revealed serious deficiencies. Each language group in the CBC-IS developed its own objectives and operated as an autonomous unit rather than as a unit of a coherent whole. He also discovered that a number of heads of operations were foreign nationals or recently naturalized immigrants, who lacked the necessary background to interpret Canada's traditions and to analyze her foreign policy.[264] As a result of Desy's recommendations, the independence of language sections was curtailed and a head of Policy Coordination was made responsible for the policy of the news section. The Political Co-ordination section, under the leadership of L.A.D. Stephens, was responsible for giving CBC-IS guidance and information on international events.[265] By such a division of labour, it was possible to have more controlled news broadcasts which reflected the Canadian foreign policy and which took into account the existing conditions in the countries where the broadcasts were received.

Desy's evaluation initiated a study on the objectives of the international broadcasts. A committee consisting of representatives from the CBC, the departments of External Affairs, Trade and Commerce and Immigration, met a number of times to define

---

[262]*Ibid.* pp. 11-12.
[263]*Ibid.* p. 13.
[264]*Ibid.*
[265]*Ibid.*

more clearly the purposes of the International Service. They agreed on the following objectives:[266]

a) to secure general political and social good will and understanding for Canada, in European, Latin American and Commonwealth countries;

b) to project Canada abroad by showing the Canadian life and culture;

c) to provide a reliable source of international news for the people of the Soviet Union; to counteract communist propaganda about conditions in Western countries and about the alleged warlike intentions of these countries; and, through reliable news, factual information and a vigorous statement of views on current topics, to encourage the Soviet people both to question what their government told them and eventually to oppose the aggressive policies of the Soviet government...

d) to provide a reliable source of news to people in Poland, Czechoslovakia and East Germany and to keep alive these contacts with and desire for Western democratic life and thus to frustrate, in whatever measure possible, the efforts of the USSR to dominate them;

e) to assist Canadian trade and commercial relations and,

f) to assist in encouraging emigration of suitable people to Canada from Europe.

The Committee was realistic in assessing the possibilities of achieving the listed aims. As far as the broadcasts to Eastern Europe were concerned, the Committee fully agreed that the broadcasts to the people of the Soviet Union, Poland, Czechoslovakia and East Germany, were useful in demonstrating Canadian values and the Canadian way of life, for there was considerable sympathy for the West among the peoples of these countries.

The Committee emphasized the clear distinction between the satellite countries and the Soviet Union on one hand, and the distinction between the people of the satellite countries and the communist regimes of these countries. Although the promotion of trade and emigration were two items singled out by the Commit-

---

[266]A Report for the Special Cabinet Committee from the Special Committee of Officials on International Broadcasting Policy, May 17, 1954, DEA file #50182-40, DEA.

tee, it was clear that little could be done to promote these items by the use of broadcasts.[267] The Committee recommended that funds from the broadcasts aimed at the United Kingdom, Italy, the Netherlands and the Scandinavian countries be diverted to support programmes destined for Eastern Europe.[268]

Changes in Guidelines, 1956

With the appearance of a relaxed atmosphere initiated by Khrushchev in the Soviet Union and in her satellites, Canada, along with her allies, began to modify the objectives and the methods of presenting CBC-IS broadcasts. The main object of the CBC-IS in Eastern Europe was to project Canada to the peoples of the Soviet Union and to those of Eastern Europe.[269] The CBC-IS was directed to deliver the broadcasts in a restrained and moderate tone using clear and vivid language. The revised guidelines recommended that the broadcasts should show respect for foreign "listeners'" intelligence, common sense and national feeling. Every opportunity was to be taken to interview visitors from the Soviet Union and from her satellites. Although the opinions of the ethnic groups were to be respected, at no time was the CBC-IS to be their vehicle of propaganda. Again the guidelines emphasized the fact that the radio programmes were not to foment discontent among the peoples of the Soviet Union and her satellites, but rather to promote closer relations between Canadians and the peoples of Eastern Europe. It was felt that such presentations would help to create a sense of reliability, balance and objectivity of the news service.[270]

Commentaries were to be given from a Canadian point of view. Since many Europeans were not well acquainted with the operation and the work of the United Nations, of NATO and the role of the British Commonwealth, some effort was to be made to inform the people of the Soviet Union and her satellites about

[267]*Ibid.* p. 2.

[268]*Ibid.* p. 4.

[269]"Principles of Broadcasting to Soviet and Satellite Countries, CBC-IS Operation," September 24, 1956, RG 25 G. 2, vol. 2204, file #9901-1-40, National Archives of Canada (thereafter referred to as NAC).

[270]*Ibid.* p. 2.

these topics. Although the broadcasts of the CBC-IS were discouraged from dwelling too long on the internal affairs of the Soviet Union, yet at the same time they were urged to provide authentic reporting of events or conditions misrepresented by the Soviet authorities or those of her satellites.[271]

The 1956 guidelines also contained specific directives dealing with the Russian, Ukrainian, Polish, Czech and Slovak broadcast services. This monograph is devoted to Canada's relations with Eastern Europe; nevertheless, Canada's relations with the Soviet Union, particularly those aspects related to broadcasts, is given a brief treatment here in order to contrast and compare the CBC-IS broadcasts to Russia with those to her satellites.

Russian Broadcasts

CBC-IS inaugurated its daily broadcasts in Russian in February, 1951. The objectives of these broadcasts were as follows:

a) to give the Russian people a true, comprehensive and objective view of world events;

b) to strive constantly to identify communism as an instrument of Soviet imperialism;

c) to appeal to the national self-respect of the subject people without attempting to incite them to revolt;

d) to unmask the hypocrisy of communist "democracy" in elections, trade unions, labour camps and religion as well as the hypocrisy of the Soviet "peace" propaganda and its inconsistency with the aggressive foreign policy, rearmament and its concentration on heavy industry to the detriment of the Soviet standard of living;

e) to correct misrepresentations;

f) to remind the listeners living under the communist tyranny, that although Western countries do have many social, economic and political problems, the lives of their citizens are not dominated by police, arbitrary law, official kidnapping, "trials" without benefit of justice.[272]

---

[271]*Ibid.*, pp. 3-4.

[272]Department of External Affairs to Dr. Augustin Frigon, general manager of the CBC, May 27, 1950, DEA file #9901-040, DEA.

With the coming of a limited detente in 1956, these objectives were modified considerably. Now the CBC-IS was reminded that the main objective of its broadcasts to the Russian people was to project Canada's image and the Canadian point of view with restraint, vividness and with respect. The CBC-IS script writers were urged to keep in mind that there have been some changes in the Soviet Union. The de-Stalinization campaign along with the encouragement of democratization and decentralization has opened the windows of freedom, be it very little. The new broadcasts began to focus on the quality of life in Canada rather than on politics of the Soviet Union. The International Service hoped that a cool, dispassionate and objective reporting would minimize the jamming of broadcasts.

Czechoslovak Broadcasts

In 1944 the CBC-IS began its broadcast to Czechoslovakia. Until the February Czech *coup* of 1948, there was a considerable amount of freedom in this country. There were political parties, an independent legislature, independent system of courts, a relatively free press, considerable amount o freedom of worship and a tradition of democracy. Therefore, the CBC-IS's broadcasts to Czechoslovakia were similar to those to Western countries. The main aim of such broadcasts to Czechoslovakia was to strengthen democracy in that country.

But then came the 1948 *coup*. Almost overnight the last vestiges of democracy in Czechoslovakia were wiped out. Instead, a rigid regime was installed with the domestic and foreign policies subject to the dictates of the Kremlin. The *coup* provided an opportunity for the leaders of other Eastern European countries to tighten their grip on their people.

The Czech *coup* forced the department of External Affairs to re-examine its policy towards Eastern Europe in general and towards Czechoslovakia in particular. To reach a common understanding, Canadian officials studied the plan of the United States.

However, the Canadian chargé d'affaires in Prague, Benjamin Rogers, advocated a strong Western economic and military presence in Europe to deter the inroads of communism.[273] With this, the department of External Affairs agreed. But Rogers went further than this. He suggested arming the underground army so that the subject people could, at an opportune time, rise up against the regime. In his opinion, such arms were necessary "to stiffen the resistance" and to encourage the establishment of an effective coordinated movement.[274]

The senior members of the department of External Affairs were alarmed at this suggestion. The secretary of state for External Affairs held that such a move would be impractical and would be construed by the Czechoslovakian government and people as a "provocative move" endangering peace. In his letter to the chargé, the secretary of state for External Affairs made a statement bordering on a reprimand. "A plan of this kind," he said, "has certainly no place in Canadian policy and you should avoid discussing it as a practical possibility with your colleagues."[275]

Rogers was not easily deterred by this rebuff. In his return despatch to the department he argued that he was not the only person who advocated the possibility of helping the liberation of East European people. Among those who supported such a liberation was president Truman himself. In addition, he stated that NATO powers had discussed, in a number of their meetings, underground resistance movements.[276]

The discussion of liberation of Czechoslovakia was shelved for the time being. The CBC-IS was directed to desist from urging people to initiate a struggle for liberation with the hope that the West would come to their assistance.[277] Instead, the people were to be encouraged to achieve a better and a freer life.[278] How this was to be done was not elaborated.

---

[273]Memorandum for Ritchie: "Policy Towards the Soviet Satellites," December 18, 1951, *ibid.*

[274]*Ibid.*

[275]A.D.P. Heeney to the chargé d'affaires in Czechoslovakia, November 30, 1951, DEA file #50182-40.

[276]Memorandum for Mr. J.B. Watkins, signed by Jack McCordick, February 20, 1952, DEA file #50182-40.

[277]"Principles of Broadcasting to Soviet and Satellite Countries, CBC-IS Operations", September 24, 1956, RG. 25, G.2, vol. 2204, file #9901-1-40, NAC.

[278]*Ibid.*

Polish Broadcasts

The CBC began its broadcast to Poland in 1953, eight years after it initiated its broadcasts to Czechoslovakia. Poland was in the hands of the Provisional Government of National Unity (1945-1947) most of whose cabinet members belonged to the communist party or were sympathetic to it. The Polish regime came into power in 1947 after a rigged election, characterized by bribery and coercion.

The nature of the CBC-IS broadcasts to Poland was discussed in three separate Standing Committees of the External Affairs.[279] In the meeting of May 30, 1951, John Decore, a Liberal member of parliament for Vegreville, Alberta, emphasized that there was a strong underground movement in Poland which, in his opinion, should be supported.[280] Almost three years later at the Standing Committee held on March 12, 1953, Decore again brought up the subject of broadcasts to Poland, arguing that the existing Russian broadcasts were not well received by Poles. He suggested that the Poles were too nationalistic to accept broadcasts in a language other than Polish.[281] Other members of parliament who supported such Polish broadcasts were Michael Starr, the Progressive Conservative member of parliament for Oshawa and George Drew, the leader of the Progressive-Conservative party.

The initial directive for the CBC-IS broadcasts to Poland included an encouragement for an alternative form of government "whenever a true opportunity offers." The Canadian chargé d'affaires in Warsaw was shocked by this clause and demanded that it be eliminated from the Canadian broadcasting policy.[282] The under-secretary of state for External Affairs pointed out to the chargé that there was a misunderstanding for it was never the intention of Ottawa "to espouse the cause and support" any orga-

---

[279]L.B. Pearson to the Standing Committee on External Affairs, May 30, 1951, DEA, Queen's Printer, 1951, Ottawa.

[280]John Decore to the Standing Committee on External Affairs, May 30, 1951, pp. 91-92, ibid.

[281]John Decore to the Standing Committee on External Affairs, March 12, 1953, p. 163, ibid.

[282]Chargé d'affaires in Warsaw to secretary of state of External Affairs, April 28, 1953, DEA file #11747-M-40, DEA.

nization which might eventually form an alternative government; rather, it was "to keep alive democratic political theory" so that in the future Poles could not be ignorant of the elements of democracy.[283]

The Canadian chargé d'affaires in Warsaw suggested a range of topics which, in his opinion, might be suitable for broadcasts. He strongly recommended that broadcasts be given in "an honest" and in a simple manner treating such topics as Western culture and achievements in medicine and technology. Little should be said about the Polish political situation, for fear that such a treatment might hinder the relaxation of tension.[284]

Another irritant plagued the CBC-IS broadcast to Poland. Some of the members of parliament, particularly John Decore and Donald Fleming, felt that a Polish Canadian should head the Polish section of the CBC-IS rather than an Anglo-Saxon or a Francophone. Until 1955, E.C. Hamel, who was the head of the CBC-IS news service, acted as the head of the Polish section. Decore argued that the head of the Polish section should be one who is acquainted not only with the general techniques of broadcasting but has a knowledge of the language, history and traditions of the Polish people.[285] The Canadian Polish Congress supported the parliamentarians by vehemently opposing a head who had no command of Polish, was ignorant of the Polish history and its present political situation. A spokesman of the Congress pointed out that the head of the German section of the CBC-IS was a German who as yet was not even a naturalized Canadian citizen.[286] Due to these pressures, the Canadian government agreed to the appointment of a Polish Canadian as the head of the Polish section.

[283]C.S.A. Ritchie, acting under-secretary of state for External Affairs, to the Canadian legation in Warsaw, May 15, 1953, ibid.

[284]Tom Carter, chargé d'affaires in Warsaw, to the secretary of state for External Affairs, April 28, 1953, ibid.

[285]Minutes of Proceeding on Broadcasting, the Standing Committee on External Affairs, Queen's Printer, May 10, 1955, Queen's Printer, Ottawa.

[286]Captain S. Sznuk, CBC, vice president of the Polish Congress, to James J. McCann, minister of National Revenue, March 31, 1955, Ethnic Archives, PAC.

Ukrainian Broadcasts

Lobbying for the opening of the Ukrainian section was better organized than the lobbying for the Polish section. Pressure to open this section came from various quarters. The Ukrainian Canadian Committee (UCC), a well-organized group, exerted a considerable amount of pressure on the government. It received active support from John Decore and from the Canadian League for Ukrainian Liberation which collected some 11,741 signatures for the establishment of such a section.[287]

Politically, the request of the Ukrainian Canadian Committee, representing some 350,000 Ukrainian-Canadians, could not be treated lightly. In many constituencies the vote of the Ukrainians determined the outcome of the constituency election. The leaders of the Ukrainian Canadian Committee claimed that some 40 million Ukrainians awaited these broadcasts. According to this committee, the Russian broadcasts were not reaching the people of Ukraine or Ukrainian people living in the other Republics of the Soviet Union because of jamming. And even though these broadcasts did reach Ukraine, many Ukrainians closed their receiving sets when they heard the Russian language. John Decore pointed out that one of the most effective means of checking the expansionist forces of Soviet imperialism was to befriend the Soviet minorities, particularly the Ukrainians who constituted one of the most numerous and most active groups in underground resistance.[288]

Among the senior officials of the department of External Affairs opposing the opening of a Ukrainian section were Jack McCordick and Jack Watkins, recognized linguists. The two argued that the Russian language could be understood by all educated Ukrainians.[289] McCordick held that the very existence of Ukrainian broadcasts could be interpreted as a support for a separate Ukrainian state, which according to his view, was contrary to the Canadian foreign policy. R.A.D. Ford, an expert in Russian language, and Pearson, the secretary of state for External Affairs,

---

[287]Memorandum for Mr. Ritchie, "Ukrainian Broadcasts by the CBC-IS" prepared by J.B.C. Watkins, DEA file #50182-40, DEA.

[288]Memorandum for the minister, October 25, 1951, *ibid.*

[289]*Ibid.*

did not agree with McCordick's contention. Pearson pointed out that the Russian government encouraged Ukrainian language and culture as a deliberate part of its policy towards minority groups.[290] Ira Dilworth, CBC-IS director supervisor of the International Service also favoured Ukrainian broadcasts.[291]

The Ukrainian section of CBC-IS was inaugurated on July 1, 1952 with brief statements from L.B. Pearson, Ukrainian clergymen and Michael Starr, a Ukrainian member of parliament. Pearson noted in his opening remarks that the official Canadian policy of foreign broadcasts was to inform the Ukrainians in the Ukraine about the Canadian way of life and to furnish them with the true facts about world events.[292] The clergymen made innocuous remarks. But it was Michael Starr who deviated from the government guidelines when he said:

> We, Canadian Ukrainians, deplore that you, our dear brothers, Ukrainians in Ukraine, do not have the right to a full political national and personal life such as we enjoy in Canada. But do not lose courage, brothers, for the free world has not forgotten you. The time will come when the spirit of freedom will penetrate the Iron Curtain of oppression, the prison of nation will crumble and the regime of terror will disintegrate under the blows of the victorious forces of freedom and democracy.[293]

Little could be done to the delivered script, but subsequent scripts to Ukraine were closely screened. Such words as "barbarous", "usurpers" and "plunderers" referring to the Soviets were eliminated. For the most part, the Ukrainian scripts were of high calibre. An exception to this record came when the head of the Ukrainian section, Gordon Panchuk, tailored his broadcasts to sat-

---

[290]Memorandum for the minister, "Policy of the CBC-IS," December 14, 1951, *ibid*.

[291]Memorandum for the minister, October 25, 1951, *ibid*.

[292]Broadcast of l.B. Pearson's inauguration of the CBC-IS Ukrainian Service, July 1, 1952, RG/25/G2/2216, PAC.

[293]"What is the situation with regards to the Voice of Canada," *Homin Ukrainy*, February 7, 1959, quoted in B.J. Hibbitts, "The CBC International Service as a Psychological Instrument of Canadian Foreign Policy in the Cold War, 1948-63," Carleton University, 1981.

isfy his Canadian and American Ukrainian supporters.[294] His resignation in 1956 provided a sigh of relief to the Canadian officials.

Evaluation of the CBC-IS Broadcasts to Eastern Europe

Critics of the CBC-IS contended that the CBC-IS system was an expensive luxury which Canada could not afford. They also pointed out that the BBC, the VOA, Radio Free Europe, Radio Vatican, Radio Madrid and RIAS (West Germany) were beaming the same messages Canada attempted to convey. Taking BBC alone, the critics noted that this British overseas system operated on 37 or 38 transmitters and used approximately 85 to 90 frequencies broadcasting in some 40 different languages. On the other hand, the CBC-IS operated on only two transmitters using two frequencies and broadcasting in fifteen languages.[295] These critics went on to maintain that the BBC and the VOA could more effectively reach more people than the CBC-IS.

Supporters of the CBC-IS countered the argument of size by pointing out that the quality of broadcasts was much more important than the number of people the broadcasts reached. More importantly, only the CBC-IS could impart to the listeners information on Canadian politics, economics and culture. The use of either the BBC or the VOA to transmit Canadian content would confirm the impression that Canada was a mere appendix of either Great Britain or the United States. Even the BBC and the VOA held that the CBC-IS broadcasts were useful and should be continued.[296]

A number of critics questioned the effectiveness of all broadcasts claiming that the persistent jamming made the broadcasts futile. They referred to the complete blackout in Moscow in various industrial areas of the Soviet Union. According to sources there were 1.3 to 3.5 million short wave receivers in the Soviet Union, but the persistent jamming made listening to foreign broadcasts difficult.[297]

---

[294]Ukrainian Service, CBC-IS, August 23, 1957, DEA file #11747-1-40, DEA.

[295]Jean Desy, director general, International Service of the CBC, before the Standing Committee on External Affairs, March 12, 1953, Queen's printer, 1953.

[296]*Ibid.* pp. 140-141.

An estimate of the number of radio-receivers in satellite countries was based on a number of sources. Among these were the mission reports, interviews with the refugees who reached the West and letters mailed to the Canadian missions in Poland and Czechoslovakia. According to these same sources there was little jamming in Czechoslovakia prior to 1948. In Poland there was considerable amount of jamming up to 1956, but with the coming of Gomulka such jamming virtually disappeared.

The very fact that the Soviet Union and her satellite governments spend millions of dollars to jam Western broadcasts indicates that these broadcasts were effective. Communist regimes were concerned with the impact of these broadcasts on the people they governed. In fact the very jamming provided the people further evidence of the "prison-like" atmosphere of the satellite countries.[298]

Czechoslovakia remained the best country through which the evaluation of CBC-IS broadcasts were made. In 1947, a year before the Czech *coup*, some 4,000 letters were received from listeners of the broadcasts. Even after 1948, some 150 letters were received by the Canadian mission in Prague. The Canadian mission mailed schedules of Canadian broadcasts to the Czechs who wanted them. This, however, was discontinued in 1952 because the lives of the Czech citizens were thought to be endangered by such letters. Some of the Czechs and Slovaks requested that the mailing of the schedules to be continued despite the risk of being detected and persecuted.[299]

Hard statistics are difficult to obtain on the number of listeners in Poland. But the defectors from Poland and other East European countries testified to the popularity of the Canadian broadcasts and their effectiveness. However, Jack McCordick, who served many years in various East European countries, and who was seconded to the CBC-IS for a number of months argued that the CBC-IS could be more effective if it articulated its aims more clearly to East Europeans. In his opinion, the CBC-IS continued to

[297]Facts bearing on the nature of the VOA (VOA) audience in the USSR, February 11, 1954, DEA file #50182-40, DEA.

[298]"An Evaluation of the Effectiveness of Broadcasts to Iron Curtain Countries," by the International Service, February 11, 1954, *ibid.*

[299]*Ibid.*

transmit a confused message to her friends, to the neutrals, and to her enemies. McCordick maintained that the CBC-IS should be honest and frank in saying that it wanted to help to overthrow the existing regimes by means of selected propaganda. There was no purpose in attempting to camouflage the work of the CBC-IS under the guise of portraying Canada abroad in a favorable light.

Chapter IX

Canadian Representatives in Eastern Europe

During the inter-war period, Canada was represented by Great Britain in the Soviet Union and in East European countries. These countries had consular services in Canada. There was a change during World War II as Canada agreed to establish her own mission in the Soviet Union and appointed a representative to the governments-in-exile. Dana L. Wilgress headed the Soviet mission consisting of Jack McCordick, Arnold Smith and R.M. Macdonnell. Canada also established a link with three East European countries, Poland, Czechoslovakia and Yugoslavia by appointing General P. Vanier a minister to their governments-in-exile. When Vanier was given a new assignment his post was left in the hands of a succession of chargé d'affaires, Pierre Dupuy, T.H. Stone and J.K. Starnes.

When the war ended Canada decided to continue her representation with these three countries. Since Hungary, Bulgaria and Romania collaborated with Nazi Germany during the War, they did not establish governments-in-exile in London, England. Technically Vanier continued to represent Canada's interests in Poland, Czechoslovakia and Yugoslavia until Canadian missions were established. As soon as the War was over, the Czech government invited Canada and other Western countries to establish diplomatic missions in Prague.[300] The Canadian government was anxious to do so but declined this invitation on grounds that it did not have manpower to send a representative to Prague at that time. Some prominent individuals were approached but for one reason or another they declined or did not reach the short list. After dipping into the diplomatic reservoir, the Canadian government agreed in February, 1948, to the appointment of R.M. Macdonnell as the head of the Canadian mission on the level of a minister.[301] Before his appointment took effect, the Czech *coup*, January 20,1948, took place. The Canadian government decided against having Macdonnell represent Canada at this level because it could be interpreted by the communist regime in Prague as a sign of acceptance of the *coup*. Both the Prague and the Warsaw diplomats were appointed on the level of chargés d'affaires.[302]

On May 7, 1947, the Canadian government opened its first mission on the Polish soil appointing K.P. Kirkwood as a chargés d'affaires pending his raising to the level of a minister. The appointments of such levels for both the Canadian representative in Prague and in Warsaw was approved by the cabinet on February 12, 1948,[303] but the Czech *coup* and the unresolved detention of the Polish art treasures made the Canadian government postpone raising the mission representatives to ministers.[304]

Kirkwood was annoyed when he heard of the postponement particularly in the light of the fact that Ottawa appointed a representative to Yugoslavia at the level of a minister. He argued that Ottawa's decision not to elevate the status of appointment would further aggravate Canadian-Polish relations.[305] The under-secretary of state for External Affairs admitted that Kirkwood's and the Polish government's disappointment was a legitimate one, which, he said, would be rectified at an appropriate time.[306]

[300]Chargé d'Affaires to allied governments to the secretary of state for External Affairs (hereafter noted as SSEA), February 27, 1945, Department of External Affairs files (hereafter DEA), file #11564-40.

[301]L.B. Pearson to SSEA, February 10, 1948. DEA files #9390-K-40, National Archives of Canada (hereafter noted as NAC).

[302]SSEA to the Charge d'Affaires in Prague, March 16, 1948, *ibid.*

[303]Memorandum for SSEA from L.B. Pearson, February 10, 1948; noted by Louis St. Laurent, February 12, 1948.

[304]SSEA to the Charge d'Affaires in Poland, March 16, 1948, *ibid.*

[305]K.P. Kirkwood to L.B. Pearson, June 30, 1948, *ibid.*

[306]L.B. Pearson to Kirkwood, July 14, 1950, *ibid.*

It wasn't until May 1960 that the status of the Polish legation was raised, this time to that of an embassy with G.H. Southam as the first Canadian ambassador to Poland. The return of the two trunks containing the Gutenberg Bible, crowning sword, Chopin manuscripts and crown jewels were returned to Poland in 1959 followed by the release of the Polish historical tapestries the following year. The Canadian representative at the legation in Prague was raised to the level of a minister in 1960; two years later it received the same status as the Polish legation in Warsaw and Jack McCordick became the first Canadian ambassador to Czechoslovakia.[307]

The arguments for raising the status of the Canadian legation in Prague to that of an embassy included the growing importance of Czechoslovakia as a trading partner; the increasing concern of Canadian-Czechoslovakian claims in Czechoslovakia and Czech assets held by the Canadian Custodian of Enemy Property; the need of facilitating reunions of Czech families with their relatives living in Canada; and the increasing political interest of Czechoslovakia in Western oriented policies including the 18 Nation Disarmament Committee.[308] Many of the same arguments were voiced in the cabinet when the issue of raising the Canadian legation in Poland to that of an embassy were discussed.

The raising of the status of Canadian legations in Poland and Czechoslovakia did not cause a ripple in the Canadian media. But when Ottawa announced the appointment of a minister to Belgrade, newspaper editorials expressed their disappointment. One of the daily newspapers, *Montreal Gazette*, January 3, 1948, questioned the decision of Canada opening a mission in a communist satellite which, in the opinion of the newspaper editor, was of little interest to Canadians. The Canadian government countered the criticisms of the newspapers by pointing out that it was merely following its foreign policy towards East European countries with which she had relations during the War years. Yugoslavia became increasingly important to the West when Tito's rift with Stalin occurred. Canada raised the status of the Canadian legation in Belgrade in 1951 to that of an embassy with James Scott Macdonald as the first ambassador.[309]

---

[307]Cabinet conclusion, July 3, 1962. DEA files # 939-AD-40, NAC.
[308]Memorandum to the Cabinet, April 4, 1962. *ibid.*

For each of the representatives, the department for External Affairs outlined in its Letters of Instruction, the general foreign policy of Canada towards each of the East European country.[310] Most of the directives were the same for all legations as they were encouraged to re-establish trade relations with these countries even though the import-export trade with Eastern Europe was never very significant. Each mission was urged "to exchange views and information on problems of external relations of common concern." The Canadian legations were required to provide "accurate appreciation of the political and economic structures" of each of the satellites as bases for "anticipation" of future developments. The most important directive was for each legation to maintain and strengthen "respect and mutual understanding" between the people of Canada and the people of the country concerned so as "to develop the friendliest relations" between Canada and each of the East European states. Of a specific nature, the instruction pointed out to each legation some of the bilateral issues that Canada was facing; for instance the detention of the Polish art treasures, the Czechoslovakian claims and the return of Yugoslav Canadians. In dealing with all these issues, the members of the legations were to present "a true picture of Canada and Canadian interests."[311]

Instructions from the department of External Affairs were guidelines for diplomats in their missions. Although Canada had developed a remarkably efficient foreign service, she lacked expertise on Eastern Europe. Diplomats learned on the job as they were shifted from one East European post to another. Jack McCordick served in the Canadian missions in Moscow, Prague, Belgrade and travelled on Canadian business to Budapest and Warsaw. A.F. Hart served in Poland, Czechoslovakia, Yugoslavia and the Soviet Union. Arnold Smith served in the Soviet Union and Poland. Robert Ford served in Yugoslavia and in the Soviet Union. Of the many who served in the East European posts McCordick, Smith and

---

[309]SSEA to the Canadian embassy in Yugoslavia, July 4, 1951, DEA files #9832-R-40.

[310]From the under-secretary of state for External Affairs to the Canadian legations in Prague, Warsaw and Belgrade; August 4, 1950; DEA files #4900-C-13-40 and 4900-C-9-40. NAC.

[311]Ibid.

Ford had a command of a number of European languages. McCordick, spoke Russian, German and French and Ford spoke and wrote in Russian and French. Some of the Canadian diplomats learned East European languages while they served abroad.

Whatever linguistic abilities they possessed, they developed a surprisingly knowledge of the economic, political and social conditions of the people of the country they were in. In many instances they made decisions whenever and wherever conditions warranted. McCordick, puts his observations in this manner: "We of course wrote a lot of our own instructions. In other words we took [the] initiative. We decided that here is something that can and should be done; it's in Canada's interest and we would feel our way. Sometimes we would put it up to Ottawa. We would say this is something that can be either approved or knocked down, or we would be quietly working on it and sending back [reports to Ottawa] and get[ing] a reaction."[312]

Unlike most of the West European countries where accommodations for the members of the legation and chancery space were easier to come by, East European countries mired by bureaucracy were slow in providing buildings for the diplomats. Canadians were fortunate to receive generous help from the British legations. It was the British who provided Dana L. Wilgress and his staff housing when they arrived in 1943 in Kuibyshev, the temporary wartime capital.[313] In Belgrade the Canadian legation used the facilities of the British embassy to store their confidential documents.[314] In Warsaw, Belgrade and Prague the British embassy showed the members of the Canadian legation documents that were sent to the governments of the British Commonwealth.

East European posts were labelled as hardship posts. In Czechoslovakia the Canadian legation worked for three months out of hotel space with the sitting room serving as a chancery. After months of searching and negotiating with the Czech government officials a suitable building was found. The members were happy to move into the renovated building after being cooped in

---

[312]Author's interview with Jack McCordick, December 18, 1984.

[313]*Dana Wilgress Memoires,* The Ryerson Press, 1967, p. 1218.

[314]Author's interview with Jack McCordick, December 8, 1984.

the Ambassador Hotel and labouring "for nearly three months under sweat-shop conditions."[315]

In Poland, K.P. Kirkwood and his skeleton staff worked in a badly damaged hotel in Warsaw. It took time and effort to bring some semblance of order to the war- torn city. About 85% of the city was destroyed by the Germans. Even four years later large portions of the city remained in ruins. A.F. Hart who served in the Canadian legation in Warsaw from 1951 to 1953 observed that "the reconstruction process was so intense that even on a nice summer day there would be a kind of haze of dust overlying the city."[316]

Besides the many inconveniences and bureaucratic snags associated with their physical well-being, the members of the legations had other hardships. They encountered great difficulties in arranging meetings with members of various ministries. The communist regimes influenced by the Kremlin refused to have meaningful dialogues with foreign diplomats. During the two years (1951-1953) Hart was in Poland he managed to have but five contacts with the Polish foreign ministry officials.[317] After the *coup* the Czech officials shied away from dialogues with Western legations.

In Poland, Yugoslavia and Czechoslovakia the legation members were continuously watched. One could not travel through these countries without having a car following. If one wanted to travel permission had to be obtained from state authorities. On occasions a car with the foreign diplomatic license would be recorded at intersections by policemen. At times such surveillance bordered on the ridiculous. One of the diplomats shared an incident when he was followed very closely by a car driven by "those fellows." In an attempt to shake them off, he went into a church. One of the "fellows" went so far as to follow him into the church, sit beside him and even try to decipher what type of prayers he was saying.[318] Residences of the members of the legation as well as the chancery office were often bugged by the secret police.

[315]Macdonnell to Mathews, June 13,1947, Prague Staff file, RG 25, volume 665, NAC.

[316]Author's interview with A.F. Hart, May 6, 1984.

[317]*Ibid.*

[318]Author's interview with Benjamin Rogers, May 21, 1984.

In 1950 the department of External Affairs began a review of the usefulness of Canadian missions in Eastern Europe. There was little trade or immigration; most of the trade was carried out among satellite countries and the Soviet Union. As to immigration, the communist regimes argued that they needed all the manpower they could muster for the re-construction of their countries. Contacts with the people were marginal as members of foreign legations did not wish to place East European citizens in compromising situations. Secret police kept close scrutiny of the people who had contacts with foreigners from the West. Those who did, underwent some type of deprivation or persecution.

The expulsion of the Canadian military attaches from Czechoslovakia and the refusal of the Polish government to accept the Canadian nominated military attaché made the East European posts less than useful. Added to this serious grievance, the Polish government re-evaluated the Polish currency making the cost of operating the Canadian mission very expensive. In the review of the posts, the department of External Affairs asked its officers to assess the posts where they served. Then the under-secretary of state for External Affairs drew up the pros and cons for closing the posts. The arguments for closing the missions included the cost of operating these missions particularly the one in Warsaw weighing it against its usefulness. It emphasized the limited amount of reliable information that could be obtained by the mission. It also argued that the United Kingdom could look after Canadian interest in these three countries as it was doing in Romania, Hungary and Bulgaria. Finally, foreign policy specialists in Washington and in Paris could assist in interpreting events from the Canadian standpoint of view.[319]

There were also compelling arguments for maintaining the missions.[320] At no time, it was argued that financial restraints be the main reason for closing missions. Specific issues such as the Polish art treasures, the Czechoslovakian legal and financial claims and the re-entry of Canadian-Yugoslavs to Canada required Canadian presence in the countries concerned. The presence of western diplomats provided the people in the satellite countries with hope. Then there was the question as to the future importance of a

---

[319]Memorandum for Jules Leger, November 13, 1950, DEA files #10258-40.
[320]Ibid.

mission. For instance the rift between Tito and Stalin made the Belgrade mission, initially regarded as marginal, escalated its significance to Canada. Finally, such countries as the United Kingdom and the United States encouraged Canada to maintain its mission as a means of providing the people of communist states with hope and courage.

After a careful scrutiny the Canadian government decided to retain the East European posts. Despite some difficulty the diplomats were able to obtain useful information from other sources than the ministries. They obtained data from the American, British, French, Turkish and Australian legations. There was also an art of reading the communist press including trade and literary journals. The manner in which the journalists expressed themselves and the items they omitted provided clues for discovering what was really happening in the communist satellites.[321] Candid and friendly exchanges occurred between the Canadian diplomats and Polish and Yugoslavian diplomats at the United Nations. For instances, negotiations for the release of the Polish treasures was spurred on by informal talks between the Polish delegate Manfred Lachs and John Holmes[322] who served as one of the Canadian representatives at the UN. Than there were occasions in the post 1956 era that Canadian diplomats in Poland and in Yugoslavia had informal conversations with the people. Such opportunities occurred when the diplomat would pick up hitchhikers and strike an informal conversation with them or meet citizen of the country at a party.[323]

Legations were not only to glean information and forward it to Ottawa; they were also to influence the people of the communist countries and even the policies of Western governments. As a seasoned diplomat, Arnold Smith, put it: "An ambassador, by his prestige and ability could influence the people of the country he is accredited to."[324] He and another diplomat, John Holmes, went as far as saying that a respected ambassador could also influence the policies of other countries. They had in mind the influence of

[321]Author's interview with Jack McCordick, December 8, 1984.

[322]Author's interview with John Holmes, November 28, 1984.

[323]Author's interview with A.F. Hart, May 6, 1984.

[324]Author's interview with Arnold Smith, June 6, 1984.

Dana Wilgress and Robert Ford on American foreign policy towards the Soviet Union.[325]

There was a mixed assessment of East European posts by the Canadian diplomats. One Canadian diplomat who did not have a command of the Russian language while he was in the Soviet Union, "(he and his family) had fun for three years despite difficulties and problems."[326] Generally speaking the diplomats who had a command of the Russian language or one of the East European languages found the posts challenging and invigorating. Dana Wilgress, Robert Ford, Arnold Smith, Jack McCordick, A.F. Hart and George Ignatieff relished their experiences in the Soviet Union and Eastern Europe. They enjoyed the operas, the ballets, the trips to various parts of the country and their encounters with the people whenever and wherever it was advisable and possible. Some diplomats, particularly Ford cultivated rather close relationship with writers and poets.

Needless to say some of the members of legations experienced boredom and tension that affected not only their work but also their health. One chargé d'affaires relates of such effect when he was in Prague. "I remember in the late fall or early winter of 1950 I was having trouble with my eyes. I went to see an eye specialist in Prague who examined my eyes and said 'You're under quite a strain here, aren't you' I said 'yes.' He then said there is nothing wrong with your eyes; you need a holiday. Actually, we were going off to ski in Austria in two weeks, and I didn't have to change my glasses."[327]

J.B.C. Watkins, who spent three years as a chargé d'affaires in Moscow and later was appointed the ambassador to the Soviet Union(1954-56) sympathized with Rogers' predicament making the following observations: "many of the irritations and frustrations from which it (Prague legation) suffers are accepted as normal in Moscow where only a very few Western diplomats waste their nervous energy kicking against the pricks, and where of these the most choleric often find out too late that the only result has been to induce in themselves nervous breakdowns, heart attacks or

[325]Author's interview with John Holmes, November 28, 1984 and with Arnold Smith, June 6, 1984.

[326]Author's interview with B. Seaborn, May 29, 1984.

[327]Author's interview with Benjamin Rogers, May 31, 1984.

paralytic strokes." He agreed with Rogers that it is desirable "to hop into cars and drive off to Vienna or Geneva or Paris for relief."[328]

But the conditions in Czechoslovakia were not exactly the same as they were in Poland nor in Yugoslavia or in the Soviet Union. Despite the communist regimentation in Poland the Poles expressed themselves more freely in the open than the Czechs.[329] They did not hesitate to criticize their political masters on the buses or trains particularly if they were fortified with some Polish "spirits." In Yugoslavia, after the rift between Tito and Stalin in 1949, the members of Western legations found it comparatively easy to have recourse to the various ministries and to meet Yugoslav people while touring the country.[330]

Speaking from experiences as the under-secretary of state for External Affairs and sixteen years as the Canadian ambassador to the Soviet Union (1964-80) and two years as an ambassador in Yugoslavia, R.A.D. Ford observed that the department for External Affairs could send almost anyone to France or Italy or other Western countries, but to send diplomats to Eastern Europe one needed to find individuals with specific linguistic and personality qualifications.[331] There was a vast difference between posts in Western Europe and posts in Eastern Europe he states. And within Eastern Europe there were differences with regards to surveillance, standard of living, and housing in Poland Czechoslovakia and Yugoslavia.

---

[328]Secretary of state for External Affairs to chargé d'affaires in Czechoslovakia, November 23, 1951, file # 11564-40, DEA, NAC.

[329]Author's interview with Jack McCordick, December 8, 1984.

[330]Author's interview with R.A.D. Ford, August 8, 1985.

[331]Author's interview with R.A.D. Ford, August 8, 1985.

Chapter X

Conclusion

Any evaluation of Canada's relations with Eastern Europe must be done in context of East-West relations. In the post-World War period the Soviet Union emerged as a superpower which dominated Eastern Europe and which threatened the security of the West. The Cold War era indicated the depth of tension created by this domination and by the aggressive policy of the Soviet Union. It was but natural that the effects of this Cold War would be evident in Eastern Europe. Likewise, the thaw that developed after the death of Stalin spilled over to the Soviet satellites.

In her relations with foreign countries, Canada had always recommended that her representatives abroad do their utmost to encourage trade wherever possible. Despite all attempts of the Canadian trade commissioners, trade between Canada and Eastern Europe has never been significant, when compared with the volume of trade with Western European countries and particularly with the United States.

It was of some importance that Canada maintained contacts with countries from which many Canadians immigrated. Many nationals and the ethnic Canadians of East European background wished to retain their ties with the countries of their birth or the birth of their forefathers. Now and then these ethnic Canadians had presented briefs to the Canadian government on such areas as immigration and human rights. Cultural and academic exchanges between Canada and Eastern Europe has increased considerably in the last two decades.

One must look at Canada's relations with Eastern Europe in another context. Canada belonged to the North Atlantic Treaty Organization (NATO) whereas the East European countries belonged to the Warsaw Pact alliance. NATO, organized in 1949, was a military alliance to which Canada had contributed manpower and military materiel, not because she wished to be engaged in another war; on the contrary, Canada hoped that this alliance would deter powers from initiating conflicts. For this reason she had supported confidence-building between countries.

Although the policy of confidence-building was not fully articulated until the Conference of European Cooperation and Security took place in 1972, yet Canada did follow the confidence-building in the post-World War years and particularly after 1956, by delicately encouraging better understanding between the peoples of Eastern Europe and Canadians. One of the main purposes of the Canadian Broadcasting Corporation, International Service, was to provide information to other countries about the Canadian way of life by outlining the Canadian economic, social, cultural and political policies. In addition, the increasing number of academic and cultural exchanges attempted to erase some of the myths each nationality had of each other. It was hoped that this better understanding of Western and Eastern Europeans would inculcate a corresponding understanding of the peoples of the Soviet Union as well. With this understanding would come a reduction of tensions between the East and the West, elimination of some of the destructive weapons of war and the creation of meaningful security and peace.

Bibliography

Primary Sources

1. Manuscript Documents

Collected Papers of R.B. Bennett, Harriet Irving Library, University of New Brunswick, Fredericton, N.B.

Colonial Office, Dominion Office & Foreign Office Papers, Chancery Lane, London, England.

Department of External Affairs files, L.B. Pearson Building and the National Archives of Canada, Ottawa, Ontario.

Department of Trade and Commerce files, National Archives of Canada, Ottawa.

Department of Immigration files, National Archives of Canada, Ottawa, Canada.

Governor-Generals' Numbered files, National Archives of Canada.

Ministerstwo Spraw Zagranicznych (Ministry of Foreign Affairs), Archium Akt Nowych, Warsaw, Poland.

Privy Council Office, "Cabinet Conclusions Management Branch," Ottawa.

2. Printed Documents

Annual Reports, Department for External Affairs, Queen's Printer, Ottawa.

Canadian Annual Review, Toronto.

Canada, *House of Commons Debates*, Queen's Printer, Ottawa.

Proceedings of the Senate Standing Committee on Immigration and Labour. Queen's Printer, Ottawa.

Revised Statutes of Canada, Queen's Printer, Ottawa.

Statements & Speeches, Information Division of the Department of External Affairs, Ottawa.

Interviews by the author

R.A.D. Ford, August 8, 1985

Gary Richard Harmon, June 4, 1984

A.F. Hart, May 6, 1984

John W. Holmes, November 28, 1984

George Ignatieff, November 27, 1984

Jack McCordick, December 8, 1984

Jack, Pickersgill, May 23, 1984

Benjamin Rogers, May 31, 1984

Arnold Smith, June 6, 1984

Hamilton Southam, June 5, 1984

Secondary Sources

1. Books

Abella, Irving & H. Roper, *None is Too Many: Canada & the Jews of Europe, 1933-1948*, Toronto.

Avery, Donald, *Dangerous Foreigners: European Immigrant Worker & Labour Radicalism in Canada, 1896-1930*, Toronto, 1983.

Balawyder, Aloysius, *The Odyssey of the Polish Treasures*, St. Francis Xavier University Press, 1978.

_____, *The Maple Leaf and the White Eagle: Canadian-Polish Relations, 1918-1978*, East European Monographs, Boulder, Colorado, 1980.

_____, (ed.), *Canadian Soviet Relations, 1939-1980*, Toronto, 1981.

Davies, David, (ed.), *Canada and the Soviet Experiment*, Toronto, 1992.

Dirks, Gerald, *Canada's Refugee Policy*, Montreal, 1977.

Dreisziger, N.F., (ed.) *Struggle and Hope: The Hungarian-Canadian Experience*, Toronto, 1982.

England, Robert, *The Central European Immigrants in Canada*, Toronto, 1929.

Hawkins, Freda, *Canada & Immigration: Public Policy and Public Concern*, Montreal, 1972.

Hillmer, Norman, Bohden Kordan, Lubomyr Luciuk (eds.), *On Guard For Thee*, Ottawa, 1988.

Holmes, J.W., *Canada the Search for World Order, 1943-1957*, Toronto, 1979.

Palmer, Howard, *Patterns of Prejudice: A History of Nativism in Alberta*, Toronto, 1982.

Reid, Escot, *Time of Fear and Hope*, Toronto, 1977.

Smith, Denis, *Diplomacy of Fear, Canada and the Cold War 1941-1948*, Toronto, 1988.

Woodsworth, J.S., *Strangers Within Our Gates*, Toronto, 1972.

2. Articles and Thesis

Hart, A.F., "Eyewitness Story from Hungary," *External Affairs*, vol. 8, January 1956, pp. 339-345.

Hibbitts, B.J., "The CBC International Service as a Psychological Instrument of Canadian Foreign Policy in the Cold War, 1948-63." M.A. thesis, Carleton University, Ottawa, 1981.

Kelly, C.R.D., "Canada's Trade Relations with Eastern Europe," *Foreign Trade*, July, 1962, pp. 3-4.

Page, Don & Don Munton, "Canadian Images of the Cold War, 1946-47," *International Journal*, summer of 1977.

Thomson, R.K., "How to Travel in Eastern Europe," *Foreign Trade*, March 25, 1961, pp. 17-20.

_____, "Trading with Eastern Europe," *Foreign Trade*, July, 1962, pp. 32, 35.

Wilson, C.F., "Canada's Trade Relations with Eastern Europe," *Foreign Trade*, July, 1962, pp. 3-4.

Appendices

I. Heads of Missions in Czechoslovakia, Poland, Yugoslavia

A. The Heads of the Canadian Mission in Czechoslovakia

1943 (April) General G.P. Vanier accredited as minister to the Czechoslovak government -in-exile in London.

1943 (Dec. 30) General Vanier left London. Canadian legation is in the hands of chargés d'affaires: Pierre Dupuy, T.A. Stone, J.K. Starnes.

1945-1947 General Vanier remains as an accredited minister.

1947 (Mar. 24 R.M. Macdonnell appointed as the first chargé d'affaires in Prague.

1949 (Oct.) J.A. Irwin, chargé d'affaires.

1950 (June) E.B. Rogers, chargé d'affaires.

1952 (August) J.M. Teakles, chargé d'affaires.

1954 (Mar.) G.B. Summers, chargé d'affaires.

1957 (July) A.J. Andrew, chargé d'affaires.

1960 (June) J. McCordick, first minister to Prague.

1962 (Oct.) J. McCordick, first ambassador to Czechoslovakia.

B. Heads of the Canadian Mission in Poland

1943. (April) As in the case of Czechoslovakia, so in the case of Poland, General G.P. Vanier is accredited as the Canadian minister to the Polish government-in-exile. Following his assignment to another post, the mission was placed under three chargés d'affaires: Dupuy, Stone and Starnes.

1947 (May) K.P. Kirkwood, appointed as the chargé d'affaires in Warsaw.

1950 (Sept.) E.D. McGreer, chargé d'affaires.

1952 (May) T.LeM. Carter, chargé d'affaires.

1954 (Sept.) J.L. Delisle, charge d'affaires.

1956 (Oct.) J. Erichsen-Brown, chargé d'affaires.

1959 (March) G.H. Southam, chargé d'affaires.

1960 (May) G.H. Southam, first Canadian ambassador to Poland.

C. Heads of the Canadian Mission in Yugoslavia

1943 (May As in the case of Czechoslovakia and Poland, General G.P. Vanier was the Canadian minister to the Yugoslav government-in-exile. After Vanier was sent on another assignment, three chargé d'affaires, Dupuy, Stone and Starnes, replaced Vanier.

1948 (Jan.) E. Vaillancourt is appointed as the first minister to Belgrade.

1950 (June) G.G. Crean, chargé d'affaires.

1951 J.S. MacDonald, appointed as the first ambassador to Yugoslavia.

1957 (Feb.) G. Ignatieff, ambassador.

1959 (Jan.) R.A. Ford, ambassador.

1961 (Sept.) G.G. Crean, ambassador.

II. Documents on Eastern Europe

Sections D to J inclusive contain primary sources found in the National Archives of Canada, in the National Library and in the department of External Affairs.

D. Poland

1. A letter from Victor Podoski to Gustave Lanctot, Ottawa, August 1, 1940

I take a great pleasure in expressing my gratitude for the personal interest you have shown, and for your kind efforts to have the articles which form part of the treasure of Polish culture placed in the Public Records Building — the safest possible place for them.

Thanks to the attitude of the Canadian Government and particularly to your efforts, Sir, the Polish nation will now have its souvenirs placed in an allied shelter, after having been saved at the cost of so much difficulty and after having been carried across so many countries and so many seas.

It is understood that the articles in question will in no way involve the responsibility of the Canadian Government, since they have not been placed in its hands.

I hope that this arrangement, which leaves a free hand to both parties concerned, will be agreeable to your Government, and I beg to accept, Sir, with my renewed thanks, the assurances of my high consideration.

2. A letter from Gustave Lanctot to Victor Podoski, August 2, 1940

I have just received your confidential letter of August 1, following our telephone conversation of July 24 when you inquired whether it would be possible for me to receive in safe-keeping for the duration of the war certain documents and historical articles from the Polish Archives.

I had the great pleasure, after consultation with the Secretary of State, to place a room at your disposal for that purpose in the Public Records Building at the Experimental Farm, where these articles are now safe.

I take note of your declaration to the effect that the Polish Government assumes full responsibility for the period during which these articles will be in safe-keeping. The Canadian Government agrees to this arrangement and is glad to render that service to the Polish Government for which it has the deepest sympathy in the trying circumstances which your gallant nation is experiencing.

3. A letter from Josef Polkowski to Professor Szablowski, January 8, 1959

I, as one of the depositors of the items stored in two trunks at the Bank of Montreal in Ottawa, containing the Polish cultural and art treasures, certify that the following a statement made by a group of experts, who were present at the opening of these trunks and the inspection of their contents-when it was decided that these items require careful and immediate action regarding their conservation and because it was impossible to do so on the spot. I undertake to transfer to you the contents of these trunks in order to pass them on to public institutions and private persons who have authorized you to take the necessary action regarding their conservation.

4. A letter from Jerzy Szablowski to Josef Polkowski, January 8, 1959

This is to acknowledge receipt of your letter of January 8, 1959 and to inform you that:

(1) Due to the decision regarding the transfer to Poland of the Polish treasures, deposited at the Bank of Montreal in Ottawa, I declare on behalf of the Polish institutions and private persons who have authorized me and in my own name that I renounce also any eventual claims regarding the items which you have deposited at the Bank of Montreal in Ottawa and I renounce all claims against you regarding the items and I renounce also any eventual claims regarding the consequences of depositing them there in the belief that you have been unable to have conservation work done there because of lack of technical facilities. I am providing you with an English text of an appropriate statement in this respect.

(2) I declare that upon their arrival in Poland I will deliver the items in question to public and Church institutions and to private persons there, who have authorized me to take care of them. It

will be my responsibility to look after these treasures and to cover the cost of their transfer to Poland.

(3) I agree that photographs and microfilms of the art treasures, printed matters and manuscripts may be taken.

5. A letter from Archbishop Maurice Roy of Quebec to Premier Maurice Duplessis, January 20, 1959

I have the honor to answer your communication regarding the Polish Treasures kept at the Quebec Provincial Museum.

In 1945, His Eminence Cardinal Villeneuve was happy to help the official representative of Poland to find a safe shelter to assure the conservation of the historical treasures of his country. After succeeding Cardinal Villeneuve as Archbishop of Quebec, I did not have to intervene in this affair which had been settled according to civil law among M. Babinski, the Hotel-Dieu of Quebec and the honourable Prime Minister of the Province of Quebec.

If some person can be authorized to receive this precious deposit and to hand it over to its legal proprietor, the Church of Poland, I shall be the first to rejoice.

I am very grateful to you for having assured for more than ten years the conservation of these treasures particularly dear to our Polish Brethren.

Please accept, Mr. Prime Minister, the expression of my great esteem and for my devoted affection in Our Lord.

6. A letter from Premier Maurice Duplessis to Archbishop M. Roy, January 31, 1959

You were willing to share with me in our letter dated January 31 your worries regarding the required guarantees in case the Polish treasures would be returned to the Church of Poland.

Since you honored me by requesting my opinion I have sought additional information on the problem. I know that his Eminence Cardinal Wyszynski, the primate of Poland, is disposed to make a concrete proposition concerning the nomination of the person who would receive the precious deposit and then assure its transfer to Poland under the entire responsibility of the Cardinal Primate. I believe we would officially and obligingly, let his Eminence Cardinal Wyszynski know the time would have come to offer a concrete proposition. I guess that if the Cardinal would accept the entire responsibility of this transfer we will be in good conscience to return to him this deposit. I don't forget, however, that this deposit was not entrusted to me as Chief of the State, you may have to keep account of certain facts unknown to me.

E. Czechoslovakia

1. From General H.G. Crerar, to the Secretary of State for External Affairs, October 21, 1946

I had conversations of some length with President Benes, Prime Minister Gottwald, (Mr. Masaryk as interpreter) Deputy Prime Minister Fierlinger and Foreign Minister Masaryk, on the political side. I also had short talks with the Deputy Mayor of Praha (Mrs. Pelantova) and the Mayors and officials of Melnik and Terezin. The Minister of Defense, General Svoboda and Chief of Staff, General Bocek, particularly the latter, I met on numerous occasions. These two senior officers, undoubtedly, hold the Canadian Army and military record of Canada, in very high esteem. The British Ambassador, Sir Philip Nicholl, his First Secretary, Mr. Schuckborough, and the British Military Attaché, Colonel Mullins, were frequently on hand, and also were most hospitable. Their kindness and help added greatly to the amenities of the visit.

It seems to be the opinion of the US Embassy in Praha, as voiced to me by the US Military Attaché, (such US opinion being confirmed by later separate conversations with the British Ambassador and his First Secretary), that Czechoslovakia is definitely, and permanently, in the "Russian bag." Strategically this is certainly the case at present — as a glance of the map will show. On the other hand, the strong impression given me, and other members of my party, by remarks made by numerous Czechoslovaks whom we met, was that though circumstances presently made a pro-Soviet attitude inevitable, the general, and intense hope was that this factual domination of Central Europe (and so of Czechoslovakia) by Russia would not long continue. However, a strong Western Europe, supported by sound economic and political agreements with the British Commonwealth and the United States, seems to be a pre-requisite to any change in the present Czechoslovak attitude and actions.

In conversations, it was made clear that in the eyes of Czechoslovakians, there were, now, only two "World Powers", Russia and the United States, perhaps it would be more accurate to say "Russia and the Western Hemisphere," because Canada and other American countries seemed to be considered by the Czecks, (sic.) as in practical alignment with the United States. It also appeared to be the view that just as Canada had been, on so many vital occasions, the "connecting link" and interpreter between the United Kingdom and the United States, it was possible, given the establishment of more effective political contacts and trade relations, that Canada would some day act as a somewhat sympathetic "link" between Czechoslovakia and the United States. In any event, there appeared to be a genuine admiration of the international role, political and military, played by Canada in the two World Wars. It was accepted that Canadians had entered, and fought throughout each Great War, in support of fundamental human principles and, by the record, had done so without thought of selfish, future, material gain. To Czechoslovakians, therefore, the moral position of Canada in international affairs stands very high, indeed.

One very clear impression carried away, I believe, by each of the Canadian official party, was that in Praha is now to be found probably the most important European political "information centre." It is here that all repercussions between the Soviet, US and UK Government (sic!) policies and ambitions are most quickly felt, and most closely examined. My responsibility, and that of those with me, was to keep clear of politics and avoid discussions on international subjects while the guests of Czechoslovakia. At the same time, it was impossible not to become convinced of the key position now occupied by Praha as an international "listening post." It is the policy of the Canadian Government to keep in first-hand touch with the "pull and push" of international ambitions in Europe, then Praha should be on a high priority for the establishment of a Canadian Legation.

2. R.M. Macdonnell, chargé d'affaires in Prague, to the secretary of state for External Affairs, August 28, 1947

It is often asked whether Czechoslovakia is inside the iron curtain, and most Czechs and Slovaks regard this as an uninformed and exasperating question. Much depends on the interpretation given to Mr. Churchill's famous phrase. If it is taken to mean close political association with and dependence on the Soviet Union, there can be no question that Czechoslovakia is in the iron curtain camp, but a more usual and useful interpretation regards the iron curtain as a barrier to freedom of movement and circulation of information. In this sense, there is comparatively little of the iron curtain in Czechoslovakia.

With the usual exceptions to be found in all countries (military installations, special factories, etc.), foreigners may come and go as they please. This is also true of the Czechoslovak population, judging by the thousands to be met surging up and down the Republic by train, bus, bicycle and on foot in pursuit of fresh air, exercises and a change of scenery. Foreign visitors are welcome everywhere, and beyond sometimes having to supply the police with an unnecessarily large number of vital statistics at each stop (usually accomplished by having the hotel extract the information from the visitor's passport), foreigners are subject to no official control over the movements.

In the field of information one must consider imports, exports and internal distribution. In all three sections there is an absence of anything approaching totalitarian direction, although some selection, suppression and distortion is practised by the Government.

As regards the inflow of information from abroad, foreign newspapers and periodicals are freely sold in Prague and the large centres. Street newsstands in Prague regularly display the London "Times" and other London dailies, the Paris "Herald Tribune", "Time" and "Newsweek" and a wide range of English, French, Belgian and Swiss publications as well as those from the Slav countries. The value of such distribution is obviously limited by the number of people who read foreign languages (which in this country is rather high) and the amount of foreign exchange that is made available for this purpose. Occasionally a whole issue of a foreign publication is confiscated on order of the Ministry of Information (a strongly Communist Ministry) for having said something rude, but this is exceptional. Finally, in dealing with information from abroad, mention must be made of foreign short-wave broadcasts. There is nothing secret or suspect about the fact that for a large part of the twenty-four hours and particularly in the evening there is a wide choice of broadcasts in Czech and in foreign languages from particularly every country in Europe and from the United States and Canada as well. We have no idea how many short-wave receiving sets there may be in the country, but we do know that they are being turned out by the factories and that quite a large number escaped detection during the German occupation. Moreover the standard of living is high enough to permit the ownership of short-wave receivers by a good number of people. There is, therefore, a listening audience, though it must be of the order of thousands rather millions, and publicity is given in the papers as well as on the air to foreign broadcast schedules. We ourselves have had no difficulty in obtaining publicity in the newspapers for the programs of the Canadian Broadcasting Corporation International Service; in fact our problem has been to keep ourselves supplied with enough program schedules to meet the demand.

3. Benjamin Rogers, chargé d'affaires in Prague to the secretary of state for External Affairs, June 23, 1952

In this dispatch I review the treatment accorded to this Mission since I came here in June 1950.

Access to Officials

On my arrival I had some difficulty in obtaining an appointment with the Chef de Protocol. When I met him at a reception he suggested that I come at a time when it would be convenient for one of the Vice-Ministers of Foreign Affairs to receive me. Numerous telephone call failed to result in my being received and three weeks passed before I succeeded in obtaining an appointment. Since then I have had no difficult in obtaining appointments.

Since the Spring of 1951 all diplomatic missions have been required to conduct their relations with Czechoslovak public authorities only through the Ministries of Foreign Affairs and Foreign Trade.

Relations with Officials

Each of our July 1st reception has been attended by member of the Government; by a Vice-Minister of Foreign Affairs and Foreign Trade; and by a couple of Army officers from the Foreign Liaison Section of the Department of National Defence. A Vice-Minister of Foreign Affairs, the Chef de Protocol, and two other officials of the Foreign Ministry attended our farewell reception.

On one other occasion, about eighteen months ago, three officials and the wife of one of them came to a small cocktail party which we arranged in honour of a young secretary who was been posted to the Czechoslovak Legation in Ottawa. They had to get permission from higher authority to attend.

In March of this year and again yesterday, heads of missions were invited to attend meetings of the National Assembly where they had to make difficult decisions whether they should stand or remain seated when everybody else stood up to hail Stalin, Gottwald or Zapotocky.

Although our personal relations with officials with whom we have dealings are never very cordial, we have usually managed to avoid snarling at one another. My most unpleasant experience was with a former Vice-Minister of Foreign Affairs, a thoroughly unpleasant character, who was purged over a year ago. A good many of our conversations concern complaints about which it is difficult to be jocular. On a technical matter, for instance, concerning patents-it has been possible to carry on quite normal discussions; and my farewell visits to officials have been marked by expressing of mutual good will.

Housing

Members of the Legation staff without exception have had difficulty in obtaining living accommodation and most of them have had to spend long months in the Hotel Alcron. This has cost our Government a good deal of money and has been pretty uncomfortable for the people concerned. Incidentally, it has helped in some measure to ease Czechoslovakia's foreign exchange problems. It has frequently happened that members of the staff have found suitable vacant accommodation which the authorities have refused to let them occupy. Last year, for instance, a secretary of the Indian Embassy vacated an apartment on June 10. Mr. Williamson applied for it immediately but was unable to move in until after the middle of August, nearly six months after his arrival in Prague. He still doesn't know what rental he is supposed to be paying. The Office of Services for the Diplomatic Corps some months ago asked for the equivalent of $1,000 on account which we have refused to pay.

The Air Attaché applied several times for summer house that his predecessor had had, but was refused a "decree" for it on the ground that it was going to be used as a school. In fact, it was vacant all last summer and is still vacant.

I am sure that our housing difficulties are due partly to bureaucratic inefficiency. I gather that relations between the Office of Services for the Diplomatic Corps and the municipal authorities are not too happy and that the former has not been able to get permanent control over certain accommodation which could then be transferred from one foreigner to another. But there is undoubtedly an element of ill will. In any case we have to deal with an organization which cannot or will not permit us to occupy available housing.

Police Surveillance

The Air Attaché has suffered more than the rest of us from police surveillance. At one stage, for a period of nearly a month, he was followed pretty constantly. During the aforementioned trip to Slovakia I was followed for several day by secret police who had the effrontery to commander one of the rooms that I had reserved for our party at the hotel at Tatranska Lomnice. On returning to Prague I addressed a protest to the Ministry of Foreign Affairs and eventually received an apology.

F. Yugoslavia

1. From Ray Atherton, American ambassador in Ottawa, to the secretary of State, Washington, May 28, 1947

I have the honor to report that 500 Yugoslavs and Canadian citizens of Yugoslav origin are scheduled to sail from Montreal for a Yugoslav port within a few days aboard the S.S. Radnik, it being reported that the 500 in question are only the first contingent of a total of approximately 1,500 persons who will leave the Dominion for Yugoslavia aboard four Yugoslav ships this spring and summer.

The departure of the groups in question has been given considerable attention in the press, as have statements made in connection with the emigration movements in anti-Tito quarters and by supporters of the Belgrade regime, including its representatives in Canada. The press, including the Montreal Gazette which originally "broke" the story, has emphasized charges of anti-Tito groups that the entire movement is Communist-inspired, the most of those leaving are doing so for fear of reprisals against relatives in

Yugoslavia and that many of those now emigrating will return to Canada as Communist agents. It has also been alleged that large amounts of money and agricultural equipment are being taken with them by the Yugoslavs.

The pro-Tito Canadian Council of South Slavs, which is sponsoring and arranging for the movement with the approval of the Yugoslav government representatives in Canada, has issued statements characterizing all of the foregoing charges as "stupid lies" and asserting that the emigrants "are returning to Yugoslavia for the purpose of lending their skill and assistance in the reconstruction of the country."

About 330 of the first emigrants attended "farewell banquet" given at the Mount Royal Hotel in Montreal at which the theme of all of the addresses was fervent praise of Marshal Tito and of his government, coupled with attacks on "reactionaries." The banquet was addressed by Brnko Vukelich, acting Yugoslav Consul General in Montreal, Edward Vardas, secretary of the Canadian Council of South Slavs and A. Miosich, who was described a "Press Attaché." of the Yugoslav Legation in Ottawa but who is not on the Department of External Affairs' diplomatic list.

In reply to a series of questions, Secretary of State for External Affairs, St. Laurent, stated on May 23 in the House of Commons that his Department was originally approached by the Yugoslav Chargé d'Affaires in March 1946 concerning the granting of export permits and exchange permits for Yugoslav nationals wishing to return to Yugoslavia. Subsequently, a proposal was made by the Yugoslav Chargé for the pooling of the resources of the emigrants in a bank account to be established by the Canadian Council of South Slavs, the funds to be used for the purchase of equipment to be taken with them by the emigrants to Yugoslavia. Mr. St. Laurent stated that deposits to the account have amounted to approximately $1,000,000 and that export permits have been granted for the export of equipment to Yugoslavia in the amount of $345,918. He added that the emigrants had satisfied Canadian laws and regulations and were entirely free to proceed to Yugoslavia, but that "every effort" would be made to guard against the misuse of Canadian passports issued to members of the group who were Canadian citizens." This latter statement was prompted by a question as to whether the Government could take steps to ensure that each Canadian passport issued to the group would be identifiable if it were returned to Canada after being transferred to another person.

2. The secretary of state for External Affairs to the Canadian ambassador in Washington, October 16, 1950

No approach has been made to us by the Yugoslavs either here or in Belgrade, for economic assistance. In view of the strategic importance to the West of maintaining the opposition of Yugoslavia to Soviet and satellite pressure at as high level as possible and in view of effect which a worsening of Yugoslavia's economic situation may have on her ability to resist, it would seem to be desirable that interested countries consider what assistance should be given to Yugoslavia. Canada if invited would probably be willing to participate in discussions on this subject. The initiative would, however, have to be taken by the powers most directly concerned, particularly the United Kingdom and the United States.

While further consideration will have to be given to this problem, following remarks would seem to apply:

The extent of the Yugoslav need.

The figures which the Yugoslavs have supplied are to some extent conflicting and are certainly inadequate. Their stated requirements are presumably their first asking figure and should be scaled down on that score alone. In any event the countries which would eventually contribute should be given full information as to the scope of the disaster and on the measures of an internal nature which the Yugoslav Government is taking and intends to take to meet it.

The urgency of the need.

It seems to us that, regardless of the severity of the crop failure, there would be sufficient supplies on hand to last for some months. Moreover, Crane reports that up to $22,000,000 may well become available from the Export-Import Bank and the International Monetary Fund to get things started. If this is so, supplies from Canada under some scheme to cover the balance of Yugoslav requirements might not have to be shipped before spring. There would, therefore, be time to negotiate and no final decisions need be taken in a hurry.

(c) The financing of a Canadian contribution.

Availability of supplies would not be a problem-the items on the Yugoslav list which we could most likely provide are wheat, barley and beans-but financing would present most serious difficulties. Financing either by loan or gift would require prior approval by Parliament which is not scheduled to meet until February. A gift could not be covered by any of the existing appropriations. In any case, it is doubtful that the Cabinet would even discuss a gift on the terms suggested by the Yugoslavs. The possibility of much money being raised in Canada by private fund-raising campaign among the Canadians of Yugoslav origin or in the public generally does not appear very bright.

3. Possible invitation to President of Jugoslavia (sic) to visit Canada, Cabinet Papers, January 17, 1957

The prime minister reported that Marshal Tito had accepted in principle an invitation from President Eisenhower to visit the United States. The dates had not yet been set but would be probably in the latter part of April. It was for consideration if the Marshal should be invited to extend his visit and come to Canada.

The Jugoslavs (sic!) had taken no steps to seek an invitation but, on general policy grounds, there seemed some good reasons for extending one. Jugoslavia (sic!) appeared anxious to maintain western contacts and was in rather a delicate balance between the west and the U.S.S.R. Tito had an important influence in Eastern Europe and assisted western interests by taking an independent line to the Soviet Union. Canada's allies were doing their best to prevent him from joining too closely with the Kremlin. If Tito were not invited he might feel snubbed and some of the good arising from his visit to the U.S. would be offset. On the other hand, there would undoubtedly be grumbling from Jugoslav (sic) groups in Canada and from Catholic groups in Quebec about the treatment by Tito of Cardinal Stepinac and the relations between church and state. The cardinal was confined to his village but not allowed to take over any functions. There had been a severance of diplomatic relations with the Vatican but no indication of a crisis and, in fact, a replacement to Stepinac as archbishop had been consecrated.

During the course of discussion the following points were made:

(a) It might be indicated that the time was not suitable for a visit in view of the possibility of a dissolution of Parliament and early election. On the other hand, there would likely be just as much damage in keeping Tito out as asking him in. It would be said that the Vatican's advice had been taken.

(b) Canada had recently taken a leading part in the United Nations and there was growing participation by Jugoslavia (sic) in that organization, as witness (sic!) (by) her contribution to the UN Emergency Force. It would be difficult not to offer an invitation in terms of international good relations. The Jugoslav (sic!) population in Canada would not like it, but international needs should override their objections.

(c) There should be no great delay in reaching a decision. The new Canadian Ambassador to Jugoslavia (sic!) was leaving the next day and would be presenting his credentials in a few weeks. It would be difficult for him at that time to avoid the subject of Marshal Tito's visit to North America and there would be a good opportunity then to extend an invitation to visit Canada. In any case, the visit should be primarily to Ottawa and short but Tito might be taken to see the St. Lawrence Seaway development and perhaps the atomic power plant at Deep River. He was interested in the development of power and there would be a World Power Conference in Jugoslavia (sic!) this year.

(d) The Canadian trade position with Jugoslavia (sic!) was not very good. The country had formerly taken a fair amount of wheat but it was getting all it needed now free under the U.S. disposal programme.

(e) There had been speculation in the press and questions would likely be asked in the House about plans for a visit. In reply it could be said that the matter was under consideration but Canada has not been officially notified as to Tito's acceptance of the U.S. invitation or of what dates were proposed and information was being sought through the Canadian Ambassador in Washington.

The Cabinet noted the report of the prime minister on the possibility of inviting the President of Jugoslvia (sic!) to visit Canada when he was in the United States as a guest of the U.S. President and deferred decision until further information was available on the U.S. plans for the visit.

G. Immigration from Eastern Europe
to Canada

l. Possible Movement of Czech Democratic Refugees to Canada, n.d.
Department of External Affairs

Cabinet recently approved a proposal by which unofficial
assistance should be sought in the settlement in Canada of anti-
Communist democratic refugees. The immigrants then in mind
were particularly Czech ex-diplomats and other democratic leaders. The proposals contemplated no very large movement.

It is now known however that over 10,000 democrats have
escaped from Czechoslovakia since the Communist *coup* in that
country. The great majority are in the United States Zone of Germany. A few comparatively are in the United Kingdom Zone and a
small number have made their way to France. The opinion has
been expressed that these people present a challenge to practical
Canadian action and the opportunity for a broad decision by
which a substantial number of these people might be offered sanc-
tuary in this country. Such a decision would not only redound to
the credit of Canada throughout the democratic world but would
bring to our shores a considerable number of people who share
our ideals and who, over the years, would contribute richly to our
national life. Informal discussions on this subject have been started
among a group of interested people under the chairmanship of
H.L. Keenleyside of the Department of Mines and Resources.

Preliminary inquiries indicate that these Czech refugees are
for the most part white-collar workers, trade unionists, civil servants, teachers, professional men and the like. All share this common characteristic; they have chosen the path of uncertainty and
probable privation rather than submission. They have themselves
demonstrated the sturdiness of faith which is in them.

A discreet survey is being made in Germany by Canadian
Government officers to obtain further information regarding the
employment classifications comprised in the group. It seems certain, however, that the preliminary advices will largely be confirmed. The Department of Labour has already intimated,
informally, that it could receive and place 500 as farm workers and
200 as domestic workers. It may well be that among the refugees
there is that number of persons who would be both willing and

able to undertake such work, if only as a temporary measure until gradually they find their niches in the national economy. Similarly there may be among them some whose industrial skills could readily be absorbed. For the most part however it seems altogether probable that these people are of those occupational classes which are generally regarded as most difficult to place.

Confronting this question there are two familiar and at first sight incompatible view point. On the one hand (there) is an anxious desire that Canada should make a real gesture and proclaim, by announcing our willingness to admit these people, that Canada's faith in democratic ideals is no less than their own: that in homely phrase "a little help is worth a lot of pity." Those who take this view argue with cogency that there is danger in accepting large groups of European manual workers without a leavening of the natural leadership of democratic intelligentsia. There is here too a feeling of uneasy conscience that somehow Canada has managed to do as much as she might have done; that the particular case of Czechoslovakia presents for Western democrats an unhappy record since 1938. On the other hand is the experienced, practical and more cautious view which foresees great difficulties if people are brought to Canada without assurance of employment, which employment is only available in certain distinct lines, usually of heavy manual labour which our own people are sometimes unwilling to undertake. Adherents to this view point to the immediate political problem which arises from the possibility of Canadians being displaced by newcomers and to the fact that in some lines there is already an excess of applicants over vacancies.

All nevertheless agree that a substantial movement of these Czech people could in the long run only prove advantageous both to Canada and to the immigrants. The essential nub of the problem therefore lies in the reconciliation of the long and short term views.

Such considerations as these led the group to which reference has been made above, to certain definite conclusions:

(a) That the placing of a large number of immigrants fitted only for employment outside the Labour categories in which they could readily be absorbed, was beyond the scope of regular governmental agencies already engaged to capacity in dealing with the placement of DP's and others. This would not exclude however the utilization of governmental agencies for the placement of those refugees who could be absorbed in lines in which labour shortages exist at present;

(b) that there should be formed a National Committee for the Resettlement of Political Refugees (or some comparable title); headed by an outstanding Canadian. Its purpose would be first to arouse the national conscience to its corporate and individual responsibility towards these democratic people; second, to obtain promises of practical assistance in their resettlement in Canada; third, to raise funds from private sources for carrying the whole project to a successful conclusion;

(c) that success would depend in great measure upon the benevolent cooperation of the government with such a national committee, but even more upon the qualities of the individual who might consent to take a leading hand. It is clear that the problems, being different from those which normally confront governmental agencies of settlement, would need to be addressed boldly by a fresh mind and one charged with a certain excitement for the cause. In this regard the name of the Hon. Philippe Brais was suggested as a Canadian ideally suited to this important practical humanitarian effort if his interest were aroused;

(d) that if the views expressed by this paper were shed by the Secretary of State for External Affairs he might feel able to broach the subject with Mr. Brais.

It was thought that if the interest and enthusiasm of a group of distinguished Canadians could be engaged in the work of a national committee it should be possible in the space of some six to eight weeks to lay definite proposals before government.

2. A letter to N.A. Bulganin, Chairman, from Louis St. Laurent, the prime minister of Canada, November 13, 1956.

I consider it my urgent duty to let you know that the people and the Government of Canada have been profoundly shocked by the reports we have received of the actions your Government has taken in Hungary during the last few weeks. We have made our attitude clear in the position taken by Canadians voting for the United Nations resolutions on this subject. I wish to add my plea not only for rapid compliance on the part of the Soviet Government with the resolutions, but for a display even at this late date of moderation towards the unfortunate victims of these tragic events.

I can assure you, Mr. Chairman, that I speak for the whole people of Canada in expressing our horror at the suffering of the Hungarian people as a result of their efforts to obtain the freedom to choose their own type of Government. It is not, however, my present purpose to attempt to pass judgment on the actions that have been taken but to ask you, in the name of humanity, to use your influence to alleviate the sufferings of the Hungarian people and to permit competent international agencies and organizations to help in the urgent work of distributing food and caring for the sick. In this humanitarian work the Canadian Government and people are already giving material support wherever it is within their power to do so.

The Government and people of Canada have no desire to influence the form of Government chosen by the peoples of Eastern Europe. Our only aim is that they should be free to do so, and that the Governments so chosen should steer their own independent courses, respecting the equal rights of all their neighbors and bearing in mind only the needs and wishes of their own people in accordance with the principles and purpose of the United Nations Charter.

3. A letter from Chairman N.A. Bulganin to Prime Minister Louis St. Laurent, November 24, 1956

I have received your letter of November 13. The contents of your letter and also of your recent statements and of speeches of Canadian officials about (the) situation in Hungary show that the Canadian Government seems to have one-sided, tendentious and unobjective information about (the) developments in Hungary and about (the) position of (the) Soviet Union on this question.

I would like to note that revolutionary workers peasants Government of Hungary have shown in their statements that reactionary forces inside Hungary with active support of certain circles outside tried to overturn peoples' democratic regime in the country and establish a Horthy-fascist regime. The inner patriotic forces of Hungary came out in defence of peoples' democratic regime asking for help of Soviet troops stationed in Hungary under the Warsaw Treaty.

As concerning position of the Soviet Government on question of relations of Soviet Union with Hungary this has been fully set forth in (the) "Declaration of Soviet Government on (the) foundation for development and further strengthening of friendship and co-operation between (the) Soviet Union and other Socialist States" published on October 31, 1956.

In your letter Mr. Prime Minister you raised the question of Soviet Government giving assistance to international organizations to make it possible for them to render assistance and help to Hungarian people in food and medicine. This question is fully within (the) competence of (the) Hungarian Government. As far as we know (the) Government of the Hungarian Peoples' Republic has already positively solved this question and (the) Hungarian Government has formally informed (the) Secretary General of the United Nations about this.

4. Hungarian refugees: arrangements with provinces: report on arrivals: Cabinet Conclusions, December 5, 1956

Mr. Harris, as Acting Minister of Citizenship and Immigration, said that the Saskatchewan government had presented a plan for receiving and caring for Hungarian refugees in the province which might involve substantial federal expenditure, but which might be desirable to accept and use as a basis for negotiation with other provinces.

Saskatchewan proposed to establish and administer reception centers. The Federal government would be expect to pay $3 a day for each refugee for such time as they were in these centers. If there were any expenditures for social aid, the Federal government would reimburse the province accordingly. It was also proposed that the Federal government pay the transportation costs to these centers and from them to places of employment. As regards medical examinations and hospitalization, the province would take X-rays and give vaccinations at its expense; for the first six months the Federal treasury would pay hospital costs, for the next six months they would be shared equally, and after that the province would bear the full cost. Premier Douglas had asked that this latter feature be changed so that the Federal government pay full costs for a year, after which the responsibility would be assumed by the province.

The only really serious item in this proposal might be hospitalization costs, as it appeared that it would be relatively easy to establish refugees in Saskatchewan where there was already a substantial Hungarian community and a shortage of farm labor.

During the discussion the following points emerged:

(a) It might be helpful to re-open the federal reception centers used for immigrants shortly after the war. Some of these were being occupied now as the refugees arrived and it was desirable to get the provinces to co-operate as soon as possible, particularly as the question of hospitalization would probably arise immediately.

(b) The great merit of the Saskatchewan proposal was that, at the province's initiative, it established a provincial responsibility. After a year the welfare of these refugees would be quite clearly the concern of the province. However, it had to be recognized that unless similar agreements were made with other provinces this principle might not be generally recognized.

Mr. Sinclair reported on the arrival of the first group in British Columbia, and the arrangements made to look after them. The whole of the Hungarian state school of forestry, including faculty and students, would soon be coming to the province. The University of British Columbia had agreed to help as much as it could with this group, and accommodation had been arranged by the Powell River Pulp and Paper Company. Jobs could probably be found for most of them in the summer although the older professors might present a problem. Most members of the Hungarian State Opera Company had also indicated they wished to come to Canada, preferably as a unit. The settlement and integration of its members would obviously be more difficult.

The Cabinet noted the report of the Acting Minister of Citizenship and Immigration and of Mr. Sinclair on the arrival of Hungarian refugees and agreed, in principle, that Mr. Harris might work out arrangements with the provinces for sharing the costs of their care and welfare along the lines suggested by the government of Saskatchewan.

H. Commercial Relations with
Eastern Europe

1. Export credits to Poland for purchase of wheat, Cabinet Conclusions, January 25, 1956

The Minister of Trade and Commerce reported that, on January 23rd, Polish officials had conveyed to his department a request for an export credit guarantee to cover the purchase of another 200,000 tons of No. 5 wheat on the same terms as the guarantee already authorized by the Cabinet in 1955, that is, 15 per cent cash and 85 per cent payable twelve months from date of shipment. Half of the 200,000 tons would be required during the current crop year and the remainder after the 1956 crop was harvested. This was the only request for credit received so far this year. Poland's credit was good and current surplus earnings in the United States would be used to meet payments when they fell due. The Minister though not feeling strongly on the subject, recommended that an export credit to Poland be guaranteed on the above terms but only for the purchase of 100,000 tons of No. 5 wheat required during the current crop year.

During the course of discussion the following point emerged:

A counter offer could be made requiring a larger cash payment at the time of shipment. However, if the terms of the guarantee were stiffened, the probability was that Poland would obtain the wheat elsewhere. This would be undesirable, because Canada had large stocks of No. 5 wheat and it was very difficult to find markets for this grade.

The Cabinet noted the report of the Minister of Trade and Commerce on a further export credit to Poland for purchase of wheat, and agreed that an export credit be guaranteed for 85 per cent of the purchase price, payable twelve months from date of shipment, for the purchase of 100,000 tons of No. 5 wheat to be shipped during the current crop year.

2. E.P. Weiser, head of Europe and Asia Section to Mr. M. Schwarzmann, director of the International Trade Relations Branch

At dinner, Mr. J. Votruba, the Czechoslovak Commercial Counselor, some days ago, we discussed various aspects of trade between our two countries. Some of his comments may be of interest.

If the system of Canadian Government export credits should materialize for three to five years, they would be prepared to buy Canadian barley, raw materials including hides and perhaps 20 per cent of the total in consumer goods. They might also buy some wheat as a part of these purchases if we would press them. However, Russia supplies all their requirements at present. Votruba claimed that such credit would make Canada competitive with other countries which extend credits on goods they export. Czechoslovakia apparently extends one year credits to Canadian buyers of Czechoslovak machinery.

Votruba regretted that Mr. (Gordon) Churchill will not visit Prague this Fall and expressed his hope that a visit could be arranged for the near future. He mentioned that there has been an exchange of official visits between his country and Argentina which, in his opinion, was the reason for Czechoslovak purchases of Argentine barley. It is planned that one of the Czechoslovak Deputy Ministers of Foreign Trade (he was not yet sure which one) would shortly visit Mexico, and Votruba is trying to have him stop over in Canada for a call on our Department during which he might invite our Minister to Prague.

Once again Votruba suggested that a Canadian Trade Commissioner should be posted to Prague and this time he gave some indication of his personal interest in this suggestion. He is paid a commission for what he sells in Canada and therefore he tries to spend as much time as he can selling (sic). There is no profit for him in assisting Canadian exports to his country and he would prefer it, personally, if Canadian Commercial officer in Prague would do this work. He is rather pleased with the outlook for expanding Czechoslovak exports to Canada. They now run 10 per cent over last year and he hopes to see a 35 per cent increase by the end of the year. Footwear and automobiles account for most of this increase.

Omnitrade in Montreal now employs 20 people of whom only four are Czechoslovaks. Votruba feels they are doing satisfactory work and he continues to hope that permission will someday be granted for them to open a branch office in Toronto.

3. Trade Negotiations with Hungary, Cabinet Conclusion, October 3, 1956

Approved the recommendation of the Secretary of State for External Affairs regarding trade negotiations with Hungary and agreed:

(a) that officials of the interested departments, headed by Mitchell Sharp, Associate Deputy Minister of Trade and Commerce, be authorized to negotiate with the Hungarian delegation;

(b) that the delegation should aim at the conclusion of an agreement along the general lines of the agreement of February 29th, 1956, between Canada and the U.S.S.R., and that in particular they should insist upon similar escape clauses as well as upon an Hungarian undertaking to purchase an appropriate quantity of wheat each year during the life of the agreement; and,

(c) that the quantity of wheat to be purchased annually should be 150,000 tons if possible, but in any event not less than 100,000 tons and should be for cash.

I. Religious Persecution
in Eastern Europe

1. Religious Persecution in Communist Countries

1. One of the most disturbing aspects of the Communist regimes behind the Iron Curtain has been the recurring persecution of religious leaders. These countries have all witnessed the persecution and, in many cases, the death of religious leaders of various faiths who have opposed the Communists' desire to control the churches. Although since Stalin's death there has been an easing pressure on some parts of the population in the Iron Curtain countries, it is hard to detect any signs of a real softening in the campaign against the churches. The cases of Bishop Kaczmarck and Cardinal Wyszynski in Poland and of Bishop Stepan Trochta in Czechoslovakia, all of whom have been imprisoned or removed from office in the last eighteen months, indicates that the Governments in these countries will not brook opposition or independence on the part of church leaders. The imprisonment this year of Metropolitan Arsenije Bradvarevic of the Orthodox Church in the only communist country not in the Iron Curtain bloc, Yugoslavia, closely parallels developments behind the Iron Curtain. Where the

churches are completely controlled politically, there may be kind of modus vivendi worked out but this is inevitably accompanied by a continuing attack on Christian doctrines from a Marxist ideological standpoint.

2. There has been a revival of scientific-atheistic propaganda directed against religion in the U.S.S.R. this year. At the same time the Communist Party has recently cautioned their propagandists against too harsh or direct personal attacks on churchgoers. The Orthodox Church has in recent years increased the number of its churches in some areas and there has apparently been a parallel increase in churchgoers.

3. Canada on many occasions joined other freedom-loving nations in protesting against these denials of human liberty. There has not been an important occasion in the past year on which members of the Canadian Government have dealt with this subject, but on November 23, 1953, in a statement before the First Committee of the General Assembly on measures to reduce international tension, the Honourable Alcie Cote made the basic point that it is difficult for the Canadian Government to take seriously the affirmations of Soviet and satellite leaders that they wish peace, when they permit at the same time acts of persecution which arouse the indignation of free peoples everywhere.

2. Statement on the Observance in Bulgaria, Hungary and Roumania of Human Rights and Fundamental Freedoms, given by Mr. Hugues LaPointe, Representative of Canada on the Ad hoc Political Committee of the U.N. General Assembly, on October 5, 1950.

It is not my intention to cover again the ground which previous speakers have already traversed in supporting the Australian draft resolution. Canada, however, as a signatory of the Treaties of Peace with Hungary and Roumania, has a special interest in the issue under discussion.

The Canadian Delegation supported the two resolutions relevant to this issue which were passed by the General Assembly in previous sessions. In particular, Canada, jointly with the United States and Bolivia, sponsored resolution 294 (IV) under which the legal and procedural aspects of the question were submitted to the International Court of Justice for an advisory opinion.

On January 5, 1950, notes from the Canadian Government were delivered to the Government of Hungary and Roumania informing the Governments of the appointment of a Canadian representative on the Treaty Commissions provided for under article 40 of the Treaty with Hungary and article 38 of the Treaty with Roumania.

On April 27, 1950, during the thirty-day period allowed the Governments of the three Balkan States to appoint their representatives to the Treaty Commissions, further Canadian notes were delivered to the Governments of Hungary and Roumania, drawing their attention to the advisory opinion of the International Court of Justice on the first phase of the question and assuming, in the light of the Court's opinion, that the Government of Hungary and Roumania would appoint their representatives to the Commissions, would inform the Secretary-General of the United Nations accordingly, and would be willing to enter into consultations with a view to the appointment of a third member in accordance with the provisions of the Treaties of Peace.

In two notes, the Hungarian Government contended that no dispute existed under the Peace Treaty, and that neither the United Nations nor the International Court of Justice was competent to deal with the issue. The Government of Roumania failed to reply to either of the two Canadian notes.

The refusal of the Governments of Bulgaria, Hungary and Roumania to appoint representatives to the Treaty Commissions is of grave concern to us, particularly in view of the fact that the arbitration machinery provided for in the Treaties applied not merely to the articles dealing with human rights and fundamental freedoms but to all other articles of the Treaties where no other procedure has been specifically stipulated. The situation with which we are now confronted would mean, in fact, that the Governments of the three Balkan States, by refusing to appoint their representatives to the Commissions, are in a position to commit any breach of the Treaties with impunity. This was certainly not what was intended by those who drafted the Treaties in Paris. Indeed, to admit the contention that it is open to a party to a dispute to prevent its arbitration by the expedient of refraining from appointing a representative on a commission specifically provided for, would be to admit that any international engagement can be nullified by the refusal of one of the signatory parties to abide by its procedural provisions for the settlement of disputes.

For these reasons, the Canadian Delegation feels that the dissenting statements appended to the opinion of the International Court on the second phase of this question ought not to be lightly dismissed. A negative answer by the Court to this phase, as has been recorded by one of the dissenting judges, might "lead to the establishment, by the process of judicial interpretation, of an escape clause, available only to treaty violators, which would enable a defaulting Party to the Treaty of Peace to destroy the effectiveness of the Disputes Article and to disregard," by implication "most of its undertakings under the substantive provisions, and, in particular, to render largely nugatory the guarantees for securing human rights and fundamental freedom."

I need not add that Canada, in conformity with its consistently expressed desire to strengthen the judicial and moral authority of the International Court, accepts the opinion rendered by the Court in this matter. At the same time, the Canadian Delegation wishes to emphasize that, as the distinguished delegate of Poland has previously pointed out the opinion of the Court is exclusively a legal and procedural one, an in no way touches the merits of the existing disputes.

Turning, therefore, from the legal position to the substance of the charges made against these Governments, we have, I am sorry to say, no doubt as to the reality of these violations of the Treaties. They are particularly shocking because they infringe elementary human rights which are the basis, not only of the United Nations Charter, but of our whole civilization. Individual liberty, religious freedom, the rule of law, form the foundation on which that civilization is built. We have been deeply disturbed, therefore, at the evidence of police oppression, subversion of justice, and terrorism which has come to us from these countries. Such acts are a breach of the Treaties of Peace, are contrary to the language and spirit of the United Nations Charter, and mark a retrograde step from civilized conduct. If the Governments of these countries deny, in the face of the evidence adduced to date, that such acts have, in fact, been committed, why do they not appoint representatives to the Commission so that the charges may be impartially investigated.

Now we may have to concede that the advisory opinion of the International Court of Justice has made it difficult, if not impossible, for us to prevent the continued denial of fundamental freedoms by the governments of the three states and, in particular, to stop their calculated attack upon one of the most precious bastions of the human spirit, the freedom of religion.

The Canadian Delegation feels that we of this Committee cannot remain indifferent to the flagrant violations of international agreements, solemnly entered into by the contracting parties, and that we cannot ignore the dangerous situation which such violations are bound to create. It is our clear duty to seek whatever remedy is still open to us.

In the light of the considerations I have set out, the Canadian Delegation will support the Australian resolution. While it appears doubtful if, in view of the obdurate attitude of the Governments concerned, anything can be done to help the unfortunate victims of their oppression, paragraph 5 of the Australian draft resolution envisages a procedure under which the facts of the case may be established and publicized so that world opinion may judge for itself of the conduct of these governments.

The Canadian Delegation recognizes and commends, in principle, the motives which prompted the Delegations of Bolivia and Cuba to put forward their amendments, and is pleased to give its support to those which have now been incorporated in the Australian draft resolution. As the distinguished Delegate of Australia has already pointed out, however, the Assembly's primary duty at this juncture is to condemn the failure of the Governments of Bulgaria, Hungary and Romania to fulfil their treaty obligations by appointing their representatives to the Treaty Commissions. To go any further in the context of the question under discussion by this Committee might serve to lend substance to the charges, which have already been leveled at the Court, that, in delivering its advisory opinion, the Court, in fact, prejudging the dispute between the parties signatory to the Treaties of Peace. While the Canadian Delegation does not feel that there would have been any practical advantage in placing this item on the agenda of the Sixth Session at this time, it would not, in principle, object to the re-introduction of the item, if and when the evidence submitted under paragraph 5 of the Australian draft resolution makes it desirable for the Assembly to adopt such a course.

J. CBC-IS, Psychological Instrument
of Canadian Foreign Policy

1. "CBC-IS Operations," Principles of Broadcasting to Soviet
and Satellite Countries, September 24, 1956

The object of CBC-IS broadcasts to Soviet and satellite people is primarily the projection of Canada as part of a coordinated political offensive of the Western world. The Eastern European services should promote understanding and friendship between listeners and the Canadian people by presenting the Canadian view of international affairs, emphasizing that it is part of the Western viewpoint; by reporting events in Canada and by providing a picture of the Canadian way of life. Our principal means of expressing our criticism of the communist system should be through factual descriptions of life in Canada which the listener can contrast with conditions within the Soviet orbit.

As the Canadian service is generally only carried on two short-wave frequencies in the midst of a great volume of broadcast from the BBC, the VOA, Radio Free Europe, etc., our programmes should have a distinctive quality and appeal which will attract and hold an audience among the limited number of persons who are interested in listening to a short-wave broadcasts and who possess the necessary radio equipment. For this reason the tone of our broadcasts should not differ from that used in broadcasting to the rest of the world. They should be restrained and moderate in approach, clear and vivid in language and style and should show respect for the foreign listeners' intelligence, common-sense and national feelings. An additional factor to be considered is that the Soviet authorities have recently stopped deliberately jamming the BBC broadcasts in Russia; until jamming of CBC-IS programmes is lifted, our service to the USSR, at least, will operate under a serious handicap in the competition for listeners. A consistent, moderate, though uncompromising approach in our broadcasts may make it easier to suggest to the Soviet authorities at some future date that if they are sincere in their desire to promote good relations with Canada they should put an end to the jamming of our short-wave broadcasts.

News Service

It is generally agreed that the backbone of the short-wave service to Soviet and satellite countries must be the news. We should present a reliable, balanced and completely objective international news service to counter the one-sided presentation of news in their own press and radio. There should be no suppression of news which might put the Western powers in an unfavorable light. Indeed, the problems of the Western community should be exploited in frank discussion to contrast the freedom of the members of that community with the rigid conformity which characterizes the internal relationships of the Soviet bloc. Because it is the voice of Canada, a deliberately generous share of interesting news of Canadian affairs should be included in the bulletins. Whenever available, reliable items of Eastern European news should also be included.

Commentaries

A considerable proportion of the programmes will be commentary on international affairs. This should be given from a Canadian point of view, giving due attention to the explanation of Canadian Government policy. Good coverage should be given to the United Nations, NATO and the Commonwealth about which the Soviet and satellite listeners may not be well informed. Inevitably there will be discussion of Soviet foreign policy on which our views presumably will be of interest to listeners in Eastern Europe. When the Soviet Union acts in a dangerous and irresponsible manner, or when it tries to disguise with high-sounding propaganda actions really designed to enhance its power position, we should not hesitate to say so but should do so coolly and frankly, with restraint and reasonableness. On the other hand, when the Soviet Union acts in a responsible and helpful manner, we should be at pains to welcome the fact and should certainly not automatically question the sincerity of its motives.

Comment on the internal affairs of the Soviet Union or of the satellite states should occupy only a very small proportion of the total programme content. In any discussion of internal affairs developments which suggest a move toward a more liberal atmosphere should be welcomed and listeners should be encouraged to think of further specific concessions, similar to those which are enjoyed in the West. The theme of the superiority of the Western and the inferiority of the Soviet way of life should not continually be belabored in the abstract. In dealing with news of internal affairs authentic reports of events or conditions which have been hidden by the Soviet or satellite authorities from their people should be featured. To deal with a development in Eastern Europe which is highly significant of the local way of life, but perhaps insufficiently spectacular to merit lengthy treatment, an item should be produced on a comparable theme from Canadian life, with only a passing allusion to the Eastern European development, so that the facts themselves point up the contrast.

Projection of Canada

The projection of Canada should now occupy a higher proportion of space in Eastern European programmes. It should perform a dual purpose of promoting understanding of our way of life and our country, and of allowing listeners to make comparisons with their own conditions. In this connotation most of our criticism of the Communist way of life should be made by example alone. It should be implicit rather than explicit. The presentation should be entirely straight-forward, letting the facts speak for themselves.

Exchange of visits between Canada and Soviet Russia, or the satellite countries, should be given good coverage but should be used as a peg on which to hang the projection of Canada. We should try to obtain radio interviews with Soviet visitors for short-wave broadcasts or, if this proves feasible, for broadcast on Soviet radio.

The presence in Canada of sizeable ethnic groups from the countries to which we broadcast should be exploited although, of course, the CBC-IS should never be represented as their particular spokesman. The purpose of such programmes should be to promote closer relations and sympathy between Canada and the countries concerned and not to foment discontent against the Soviet and satellite regimes. The material successes of these new Canadians, their satisfaction with conditions in Canada and pride in their Canadian citizenship, their preservation of their native cultures and their continuing love for their homeland should all be made clear, as a demonstration of the reasons why several generations of their people have to come to Canada.

Tone of Broadcasts

If the above principles are to be followed, great attention should be paid to the tone of our broadcasts which influences the attitude of the listener.

(a) Restraint

Individuals in communistic controlled countries are subjected to a constant stream of bombastic propaganda from their own authorities and are apt to discount and disbelieve overt propaganda from the West. Our listeners should be made to feel that we are not trying to convert them, but merely to express and explain the Canadian point of view on matters of mutual interest. Generalized and over-simplified condemnations of the Communist system serve no purpose. Judgment must be made of specific issues and conveyed gently. Phrases loaded with emotion should be avoided at all times, e.g. "bloody battle," "wrath of the Polish people," "hated regime," etc. (The supervisors of the International Service may need to remind some of their talented emigre staff members that they are speaking not as Poles, or Czechs or Russians but as Canadians who are by nature considerably less emotional and who take a more detached view of events and conditions in Europe.)

(b) Vividness

The vivid concrete image should be preferred at all times to the theoretical and abstract. In discussions of international news, of Eastern European affairs, or of Canada, the facts must be encouraged to speak for themselves. Lectures and homilies should be avoided. rather than a general discussion of hydro-electric power in Canada, for example, a picture of one particular power station might be presented; rather than figures about the amount of electricity consumed in Canada, the great part played by electrical equipment in our daily lives could be illustrated. Direct evidence should be used whenever possible-interviews with people, including visitors and immigrants, actuality broadcasts, etc. The criterion for any programme should be that it is alive and of interest to a reasonably wide group of listeners. If it is dull it will be a failure.

(c) Respect for the Listeners

A continuing effort should be made by the authors of scripts to place themselves in the position of their audience and to show respect and consideration for the listeners' intelligence, common sense and national pride, and to show appreciation of the difficulties under which they live. Preaching and moralizing should be avoided. Listeners should not be told as news, facts about their own country which they know all too well such as the shortage of housing, the high cost of living, long hours of work, etc. These facts can be referred to but they should be used intelligently and sympathetically in a way which will not antagonize the listeners.

In discussing problems of a free society, we should not apologize for them or explain them away, but by describing how we are tackling them, demonstrate what is meant by freedom. Rather than condemning communist actions, questions should be asked to exploit the puzzling discrepancy between the dictates of common sense and the communist policy underlying the event. Sharp hostility should be avoided-the attitude should be that of an interested observer. Improvements in the communist regime should be welcomed and hope expressed for their extension.

The above suggestions for moderation in tone should not mean any weakening in the force and effectiveness of our broadcasts to the Soviet and satellite area. They are put forward in the hope that what the International Service has to say about world affairs and about Canada will have a greater chance of influencing the target audience.

(d) An Evaluation of the Effectiveness of Broadcasts to Iron Curtain Countries by the International Service, February 2, 1954

The general objectives of Canadian broadcasts to Iron Curtain countries have already been stated with reference to the foreign policy of Canada towards these countries. This memorandum considers how effective these broadcasts are likely to be, in view of the available evidence concerning the technical problems of transmission and the political and psychological problems of influencing listeners.

The effectiveness of broadcasts to most free countries is likely to be judged primarily by the evidence of the number of listeners and of listener interest in the form of letters. Since such evidence cannot, for obvious reasons, be procured from Iron Curtain countries as a major proof of the effectiveness of broadcasts, it is necessary to analyze information of different types about these countries which is directly or indirectly relevant to our evaluation.

The fact that there is no one relatively simple means of evaluating our Iron Curtain broadcasts and that we have to turn to arguments from general circumstances does not mean that the process of evaluation is, therefore unreliable. On the contrary we have enough information about Iron Curtain countries that a careful examination of all the relevant factors can establish a sufficient probability of effectiveness to justify the cost of the broadcasts. Even in the free countries statistics about listeners and listeners' mail must be regarded as a strong indication, not as final proof, of effectiveness and must be evaluated in the light of our general information about the country concerned and about Canadian interests in that country.

Technical Questions

It would be impossible to estimate the proportion of Western broadcasts which get past jamming stations to reach listeners in various parts of each Iron Curtain country. There are differences in the effectiveness of the jamming between one city and another, and between towns and rural areas in each country. The extent of jamming operations seems to vary from time to time. The technicians operating these stations apparently select particular programs for jamming and leave others alone, on the basis of priorities which we cannot always anticipate. For these reasons it would be impossible to suggest with much accuracy what proportion of the total number of broadcasts in all languages on all subjects reached all or some areas in the countries behind the Iron Curtain for which they were destined.

The evidence available suggests, however, that the jamming operations are not so successful that they could block all Western broadcasts in a given area for some time or that they could interfere to such an extent as to discourage potential listeners from making regular attempts to pick up any of the Western broadcasts. Whether listeners wish to make these attempts, in spite of the interference, is another question which will be considered later.

The evidence concerning the effectiveness of jamming comes from monitoring stations close to Iron Curtain frontiers, from

Western representatives in Iron Curtain countries and from defectors and escapees interrogated by Western officials. The details are assembled and analyzed principally by the British and Americans for their own information and for the information of other Western nations engaged in broadcasting to Iron Curtain countries. The results of such analysis are the most reliable evidence we can expect to have. Both the United Kingdom and United States Governments are bearing expenditures for broadcasts on a much wider scale than ours and must evaluate the results critically.

The reports we get from Canadian representatives in the Soviet Union, Czechoslovakia and Poland bear out the general conclusions mentioned above. It must be remembered that our missions are small and that it is difficult for the members of the staff to devote many hours to monitoring in the capital city or to traveling to other points to test reception conditions here. The amount of first hand evidence concerning reception of Canadian programs is inevitably limited therefore. An estimate of the reception conditions for our broadcasts over a period of time must combine reports from Canadian officials with the general evidence from varied sources compiled by our closest allies. There is no reason to suppose that general reports on reception conditions for American and British broadcasts are not valid for Canadian broadcasts also.

Political and Psychological Questions-General

The expenditure on jamming is a good indication not only of the number of possible listeners but also of the fear with which Iron Curtain authorities regard the possible political impact of these broadcasts on listeners. These authorities not only jam broadcasts. They listen to some of them, for their own information and in order to reply in their own press or radio. It is a reasonable assumption that, if Western broadcasts, because of basic content or method of presentation, seemed unlikely to have much effect on the population, the authorities behind the Iron Curtain would not bother with large scale jamming operations.

Political and Psychological Questions — Satellites

It is much easier to judge the effectiveness of Western broadcasts to the satellites. In the Soviet Union one can only say with any certainty that there is a potential audience and a possible political need on the part of listeners. In the satellites there is enough evidence to warrant the conclusion that there is an actual audience of some size and an evident political need for the broadcasts. Information from a number of sources makes it clear that in each of the three satellite nations to which Canadian broadcasts are directed, East Germany, Poland and Czechoslovakia, there is a large part of the population strongly opposed to the Communist regime and hostile to the Soviet Union. These people have no means of getting reliable news, moral encouragement and analysis of current international developments other than by the foreign broadcasts. In the general Western effort of psychological defence against the Soviet Union, it is as important to keep our friends informed and encouraged as it is to attempt to convert our enemies.

The amount of opposition to Communism and dislike of the Soviet Union has an unsettling effect on Party members in the satellites and provides the Western broadcasters with good opportunities for exerting some influence. The number of "Titoists," opportunists and deviationists in satellite Communist Parties is probably extensive. The VOA evaluation staff has produced a detailed study of satellite mentalities based on interviews with about 100 refugees from each of the following satellites: Czechoslovakia, Poland and Hungary. This study along with other detailed evidence from refugees and reports from Western diplomats makes it abundantly clear that there are numerous possibilities for extending Western influence and that Western broadcasts are a major political factor in the satellites.

So far as Canadian broadcasts are concerned, the best area in which to judge their effectiveness is Czechoslovakia. Since we started broadcasting to Czechoslovakia in 1945 there was a good audience built up by the time of the Communist *coup* in 1948. The fact that over 4,000 letters from listeners were received in 1947 and over 1,000 in the month immediately preceding the *coup* shows how extensive the audience had become.

Did this audience disappear after the *coup*? All available evidence along with our knowledge of general conditions in Czechoslovakia suggests that it did not and that with the need for news and political encouragement becoming much greater the audience may well have increased.

As late as 1950, 150 letters from listeners reached the CBC-IS. In 1952 when the practice of sending out program schedules was discontinued in the interests of those on the mailing list there were still 800 schedules being mailed to listeners in Czechoslovakia each month. An increasing number of listeners were, of course, writing to the Canadian Legation in Prague, saying that they preferred for obvious reasons not to have the schedule mailed to them. They almost certainly intended to continue listening however. There were still some people writing in 1952 to ask that their names be added to the mailing list however. At the present time, a few Czechs take the risk of coming into the Legation in Prague each month to ask for a copy of the current schedule.

Index